CLOCKS AND CULTURE 1300-1700

Money, Prices and Civilization

The Economic History of World Population

*Guns and Sails in the Early Phase of
European Expansion 1400–1700*

*Before the Industrial Revolution:
European Economy and Society, 1000–1700* (2nd Ed.)

*Faith, Reason, and the Plague in
Seventeenth-Century Tuscany*

CARLO M. CIPOLLA

CLOCKS AND CULTURE
1300–1700

W · W · NORTON & COMPANY

New York · London

W. W. Norton & Company, Inc. 500 Fifth Avenue, New York, N.Y. 10110
W. W. Norton & Company Ltd. 37 Great Russell Street, London WC1B 3NU

Books That Live
The Norton imprint on a book means that in the publisher's
estimation it is a book not for a single season but for the years.
W. W. Norton & Company, Inc.

ISBN 0-393-00866-5

4 5 6 7 8 9 0

FOREWORD

To be invited to write a Foreword to this book is as great an honour as it is a pleasure. And pleasure is always to be found on the prow of those studies, however serious and learned, of which Professor Cipolla is the helmsman. This work is in two senses complementary to *Guns and Sails*. That book sketched the economic and technological process by which Europe, a continent that had in the middle ages barely held its own, won the mastery of the world. This book attempts a deeper investigation of that theme and of the human realities involved, an investigation to which the epilogue gives memorable expression. The choice of horology as the field of enquiry was not fortuitous. Clocks are the prototypes of all precision instruments: and once they are valued as such and not simply admired as the most delicate and enchanting of mechanical toys the age of industrial innocence is over.

Clocks and Culture complements *Guns and Sails* too in a sense that is both more obvious and more unexpected: the craftsmen who pioneered the development of both guns and clocks were often the same people. If wrist-watches and guided missiles are not now obtainable at one and the same shop they still to the reflective eye disclose a recognisable cousinhood.

RICHARD OLLARD

PREFACE

In the summer of 1338 a galley left Venice bound for the East. Among other things, the galley carried a clock, in all likelihood a mechanical clock that Giovanni Loredan hoped to sell in Delhi. We know of the event because later on some merchants prosecuted claims in a court of law about the cargo (Lopez, *Venezia*, pp. 53-9). No chronicler took notice of the event in those days and modern historians scarcely mention it in their writings. Yet that was a fateful event. Europe had begun to export machinery to Asia. It was a humble beginning, but a new era was unfolding.

This is not a contribution to the history of technology. For adequate information about the technological side of the story, the reader should consult the classical works by von Bassermann-Jordan, Britten, Defossez, Lloyd, Needham, Robertson, de Solla Price, Zinner, etc. Although the machine occupies a prominent place in the pages that follow, this is essentially an exploration in economic and social history and attention is focused on people and their inclinations, on societies and their sets of values.

The period covered by this study runs from 1300 to 1700. Occasionally reference has been made to events that took place after 1700, but this has been done only exceptionally in order to clarify the meaning of previous events. Eighteenth-century developments most certainly deserve a separate and more detailed treatment.

The obligations which I desire to acknowledge here are

numerous. Mrs. Barbara Darnell carefully edited the manuscript. S. C. Ahn, F. Bonelli, Kathie Chamberlin, P. G. Coole, F. Crouzet, H. F. Deininger, G. E. Ferrari, C. Fohlen, Mimi Hartford, E. Helin, G. C. Hutchings, L. Jörberg, J. Le Goff, J. R. Levenson, Ch. Muscatine, J. Muelbauer, M. Ogata, N. V. Riasanovsky, D. S. Smith, G. C. Soulis, F. Stubenitsky, Mr. and Mrs. Wittich and many others gave me a helpful hand while I was struggling with historical, technological or linguistic problems. H. Galliot allowed me to read her unpublished thesis on the clockmakers in Franche-Comté. The directors of the *Archives Nationales* in Paris and of the Archive in Augsburg generously supplied me with important information. My secretary Franca Zennaro gave me all kinds of help. The Institute of Business and Economic Research of the University of California gave some financial support to the research. To all of them I wish to extend the expression of my gratitude. I wish also to thank John Le Suer and his family for their generous hospitality: the last part of this book was written at their house in Santa Maria, California.

A few years ago, while I was bothering my head with *Guns and Sails*, a charming lady took a helpful interest in my work. Regrettably her name did not appear in the acknowledgments of that book. To the clock all days are the same and of equal length. For men, their significance varies. This book was written in recollection of days that were too short because they were too beautiful: *ut hora, Ora, sic dies nostri*.

CONTENTS

ILLUSTRATIONS

The author and publishers wish to acknowledge permission to reproduce the graph on p. 59 which is Crown Copyright. Figure 3 on p. 113 is reproduced from A. CHAPIUS *La Montre Suisse* (Urs Graf-Verlag GmbH.) and figure 4 by permission of Dondi Horological Ltd. from H. ALAN LLOYD *Old Clocks* (Ernest Benn Ltd.).

NIHIL SINE HUMANITATE

PROLOGUE

1—A thousand years ago, most of western Europe was covered by great forests swarming with wild animals and, according to the imagination of the people of the time, with fairies, dwarfs, and evil spirits. Marshes too were numerous and widespread and in the south the malarial mosquito created around them a depressing atmosphere of misery and death. The few towns, located within the geographical limits of the old Roman Empire, looked more like villages than towns proper and elsewhere there were no towns at all but only a handful of small and dirty villages.

People were few in number, small in stature, and lived short lives. Socially they were divided among those who fought and hunted, those who prayed and learned, and those who worked. Those who fought did it often in order to rob. Those who prayed and learned, learned little and prayed much and superstitiously. Those who worked were the great majority and were considered the lowest group of all. Work was a mark of low class and the '*ora et labora*' motto of the Benedictines was not enough to ennoble a fatigue that by everybody was considered incompatible with nobility.

The state of the arts was extremely low. Most of the workers were poor and ignorant peasants. Their main solaces in life were getting drunk once a year at the village feast and taking their pleasure at night with their wives, which incidentally helped to compensate for the exceedingly high proportion of children who died in the first years of life. As for the few craftsmen, some of them moved around from one village to another offering their cheap services; others preferred to stay on a manor and obtain a piece of land in exchange for the services that they provided to the local lord or to the community: they occupied part of their time in tilling their land and the rest in turning out some utensils. The manufactures were generally primitive and crude and people looked with astonished admiration at non-European products that on rare occasion they saw in the hands of those wandering and wicked adventurers— the 'merchants'—who, having sold their souls to the devil for the money, moved around from one centre to the other selling objects both common and strange, grains, silks, spices, slaves, jewellery *et similia*.

This drab picture shows signs of improvement after the middle of the tenth century, and more distinctly so after the middle of the eleventh. Population grew,[1] production developed, and in the long run wealth grew more than population. Such processes are not necessarily linked. Especially in the case of poor economies, the growth of population may actually mean the growth of poverty. However, this did not happen in Europe and why it did not happen we do not really know. Our current textbooks of economic history have always some explanation to offer, but even when such explanations are not on the level of the old tale of the fear of the year 1000, they hardly go much further. There are some generalizations one can agree on. Undoubtedly population growth was not rapid, and bottlenecks in the productive system did not prove formidable: there was much land available for the expansion of the agricultural "frontier"[2] and there were developments in technology.[3] There was also expansion both in trade and manufacturing.

This is not the place to speculate about a problem that would need many volumes to deal with adequately, but we must emphasize one fact that was at the same time cause and effect of the development. As far as we can see, urban population grew much more than the rest. This seems to have happened not because fertility was higher or mortality was lower in the cities than in the countryside but because people moved from the countryside to the towns. Within the boundaries of the old Roman Empire, towns that had barely survived during the previous centuries grew larger and had to build and rebuild new walls around their ever-growing areas. Outside old *Romania*, new towns grew up from existing hamlets, or sprang up from the wilderness itself. Until the Industrial Revolution, there were always more Europeans in the countryside than in towns, but after the eleventh century the proportion of the urban population grew steadily and indeed came to represent the most dynamic element in the development of Western European civilization.

There are reasons to believe that what brought people to the towns were the growing opportunities available in the urban centres rather than any worsening of the economic situation in the country. In fact, I suspect that things were slowly improving also in the countryside because of technological innovation and the evolution and diffusion of the manorial system. People left the country because they thought that in the towns there were better opportunities for economic and social advancement, and this belief made them intolerant of the slow mobility of the rural world. '*Stadtluft machts frei*' was said in Germany: 'the air of the town makes one a freeman'. In more than one way, this movement resembles—as far as motivations and feelings are concerned—the migration of Europeans to America during the nineteenth century. In both cases there was the same hope of moving to a better world, more open socially and full of economic opportunities.

A large portion of those who moved to the towns were unskilled labourers, often young men who then learned their trades in town. But the general economic progress affected rural areas also, artisans became more numerous in the countryside, and at least in the more advanced regions, some villages actually developed traditions of craftsmanship. Since local demand was not enough to support more than a few skilled workers, many of these craftsmen also moved to the towns and enlarged the ranks of the urban working force.

Optimism prevailed in the towns, and it nourished both a general aspiration toward reform and a genuine desire for mutual co-operation: the first took on a religious tone, according to the prevailing spirit of the age, while the second operated mostly on the socio-political level. Guilds grew, and above the guilds a larger form of association developed—the *Commune*. These associations successfully pressed for juridical recognition from the established imperial royal or feudal authorities and whether peacefully or otherwise, they obtained independent jurisdictional powers. The victory of these associations of free men over the surrounding feudal world was the real turning point in Western European history. All that happened afterwards was nothing but the logical consequence of this momentous change.

Feudal lords and landed gentry came—or were forced to come—to live in the towns. The urban centres were filled with a large population of priests, monks and nuns. But fundamentally the towns were the domain of merchants and craftsmen, and as the proportion of the urban population over the total population grew in Western Europe in the course of the Middle Ages and the Renaissance, a progressively larger share of the total European population was represented by merchants and craftsmen.

2—In setting standards of quality for manufacture and in regulating and institutionalizing the training of apprentices, the urban guilds played a positive role in the development of craftsmanship and in the development of a class of skilled artisans. Their importance in this regard, however, should not be exaggerated. Many villages witnessed the growth of a tradition of craftsmanship without having guilds, and on the other hand it has been abundantly proved that the urban guilds soon developed monopolistic tendencies and aimed to limit rather than to expand the supply of skilled labour.

The guilds played a more important role in giving their members a feeling of political importance, a socio-political bargaining power and a social status that as individuals they most certainly did not enjoy in the feudal world. Of course one should not overestimate the 'democratic' aspect of these developments. Social differentiations rapidly appeared on the urban scene. The merchants and the professionals soon acquired a predominant position and craftsmen often learned that the merchants were no less ruthless to them than the feudal lords had been to their serfs. Among the craftsmen too, social differentiation developed and was often accompanied by conflict. In most areas landed gentry, whether of rural or of new urban formation, retained much power in towns and scarcely distinguished itself for self-restraint. Nevertheless some basic principles had been established, and when one reads that a scholar like Dante had to join a guild in order to be able to play a political role one can understand what a profound difference separated the new urban environment from the old feudal society.

The emergence of a relatively large urban population where merchants, professionals and craftsmen were both numerous and influential gave to the history of the West a characteristic imprint. Sets of values that had prevailed without opposition in the feudal world did not prosper in the new urban one. Utilitarianism and practicality began slowly but progressively to permeate European civilization. The realistic reaction of Giotto to the flat, abstract and dogmatic art of the Byzantines, the optimistic and practical spirit brought by Saint Francis to the stream of monastic tradition, were both born of the new social climate. An important aspect of the change was technological progress. This was not as rapid and as brilliant as recent enthusiastic literature may induce the uncritical reader to believe,[1] but it existed and it was substantial. From the eleventh century to the end of the fifteenth, European technology moved ahead in almost every field—in agriculture as well as in the building industry, in navigation and in shipbuilding, in the textile industry, in metallurgy, in carpentry, in accounting, in finance, in transportation, in the production of energy and in warfare. Any book on the history of technology can easily supply the reader with the details of this progress. Here I want to emphasize that, characteristically enough, in medieval Europe a considerable number of anonymous craftsmen experimented in a more or less crude but determined way with wheels, gears and screws of all kinds and descriptions. In antiquity too there had been individuals such as Archimedes and Heron who had had a taste for this kind of gadgetry, but they were odd, isolated cases and their efforts never went beyond the stage of curious experimentation or limited application; machines never became an essential and important element in the productive system.[2] Byzantium and the Mohammedan Middle East followed the Ancients in maintaining the tradition of artistic technology and in both there were craftsmen who dealt with mechanical contrivances. But the number of such craftsmen was always very tiny, while the structure of demand and the prevailing cultural values generally restricted the application of their skills to the production of extravaganzas such as carousels, pneumatic fountains, automatic flutes, etc., that had to satisfy the mania for theatrical splendour of the Byzantine and Moslem rulers.[1] In medieval Europe, on the contrary, elementary applied mechanics became the concern and the object of application of an increasingly large number of craftsmen who dealt with it not out of mere curiosity but from a wish to put it to practical use. Machines came to play an increasingly important role in the productive process.

The mills are a good case in point. Water-mills were known in Asia Minor in the first century B.C. and windmills of the vertical type were known in Persia in the seventh century A.D., but it was in medieval Europe, and especially after the tenth century, that a real boom in mill construction developed. A whole series of ingenious mechanical contrivances were devised by anonymous craftsmen to transform the rotary power derived from water or wind into a number of well-differentiated movements of hammers, presses, drills, millstones, and the like. Europe was soon dotted with an astonishingly large number of mills: small mills and large and elaborate ones, windmills, watermills both ashore and afloat, mills for grinding grain and for pressing olives, for fulling cloth and for making paper, for working metal and for brewing beer. The frequency of the family name 'Miller' and the frequent appearance of millers in old tales are abundant witness to the place that the mill acquired in medieval European society; written documents and archaeological remains amply testify to the all-important role of the mills in the

most important sectors of the economy. Clocks and automata offer another good example, and this subject will be
discussed extensively in the first chapter of this book.

The existence of numerous crowded urban centres with
relatively low standards of public health and hygienic
conditions made the European population highly vulnerable
to epidemic disease. About the middle of the fourteenth
century a pandemic of plague devastated Europe and
allegedly killed one-third of its inhabitants. Throughout
the following decades and centuries, plague and various
other kinds of epidemics were a recurrent unremitting
tragic theme in European history. As a result the growth
of population was checked. We lack precise statistical
information but it is probably safe to say that at the end of
the fifteenth century the population of Europe was no
greater than at the beginning of the fourteenth.

One of the effects of the lack of a substantial population
growth in the presence of growing economic activity must
have been a substantial increase in real wages. The economic
position of the craftsmen improved, and they pressed
strongly or even violently for a more active part in the
administration of the commonwealth.[1] On the other hand,
since labour was becoming more expensive, the pressure
to adopt labour-saving devices grew stronger and the
Europeans became more machine-minded than ever.[2]

3—When one tries to describe in a very few pages a set of
changes that took place over many centuries and trans-
formed a whole continent, one is bound to be prey to over-
simplification and deservedly becomes subject to serious
criticism. In the preceding pages I have tried to single out
some basic trends that I think were of great importance in
shaping modern European civilization. But even if one

leaves aside the question of regional differences, to which I shall return later, it is abundantly clear that the previous pages scarcely do justice to all the complexities of the changes considered. Terms such as 'merchants' and 'craftsmen' are exceedingly inadequate to represent a multifarious reality of different human and social characters. It should also be mentioned that the change was painfully slow, especially in its beginnings. Only in the course of time did it acquire momentum. This progressive acceleration was the result of the fact that, as so often happens in social processes, the change was characterized by cumulative mechanisms. For instance, the availability of able craftsmen and the existence of a developed technology in Western Europe explains the rapid proliferation of firearms as well as the improvements in shipbuilding and the expansion of ocean navigation after the end of the fourteenth century. In its turn, the rapidly growing demand for cannon, cannon balls, and anchors stimulated the growth of both the metal and the mining industries, adding new impetus to the proliferation of skilled artisans and to the progress of technology. The development of mining on the other hand, stimulated the search for mechanisms that would help human muscle power or replace it in the pumping of water out of the mines and in the hauling of minerals. Similarly, technological progress and interest in technological matters gave birth to a rich literature devoted to mechanical problems. The invention of printing, itself a result of technological progress, helped the diffusion of technical literature and fostered the pace of technological advance.

It must also be said that economic development progressively enriched and diversified social groups. Among the artisans, a group of superior craftsmen gradually emerged (think of Brunelleschi, Francesco di Giorgio or Leonardo) and separated themselves from whitewashers, stonedressers, masons and smiths. They formed connections with high circles in society and actively broadcast their interests and views. Interest in the machine grew progressively stronger and was always characterized by those feelings of practicality and utilitarianism that prevailed in the medieval urban environment. 'Without mechanical ingenuity the force of man is of small avail: in building it is necessary to move great weights; likewise there is need to draw water in large quantity and convey it over long distances; no less useful and necessary will be the construction of mills, and in some places where little water is available, ingenuity must be used to help; in other places where there is no water at all, mills must be constructed that work with the wind or by some other means'. These words were not written by a professional engineer: there were no professional engineers in the fifteenth century, because specialization had not yet succeeded in putting men into labelled boxes and their brains into strait-jackets, although the trend was taking shape. The words I have quoted were written by Francesco di Giorgio Martini (1439-1501) who, trained as a craftsman, successful as a painter, and expert in architecture, ended up by writing, in accordance with the mood of the age, a treatise on engineering.[1] It was as 'natural' for the people of the Renaissance to bother their heads with perpetual motion machines, mechanical pumps, water scoops, war machines, mills and automata, as it was 'natural' for the Greeks of Plato's day not to bother theirs. One may remember the technical treatises by Fontana (1420), the treatise *De Machinis* by I. Mariano (1438-41), the writings on architecture by Alberti, Filarete and Palladio, the work on military machines by Volturio da Rimini (1472), the *Unterrichtung zur Befestigung der Städte* by Dürer (1527), the *De Tradendis Disciplinis* by Vives (1521), the treatises by Biringuccio on metallurgy (1540), by G.

Agricola on mining (1556), by Guidobaldo del Monte on applied mechanics (1577), the *Theatrum Instrumentorum* by J. Besson (1578), the *Diverse e Artificiose Macchine* by Ramelli (1588) and the *Pneumaticorum Libri* by Della Porta (1601). If Leonardo da Vinci had not existed, the history of European technology would have been exactly the same, but his drawings and sketches witness in a superb way the extravagant interest in wheels, toothed wheels, gears and the like that took over in Europe.[1]

When in A.D. 807 the great Haroun al Rashid sent an embassy to Charlemagne, among the presents brought to the western emperor was 'a clock made with wonderful mechanical skill (*arte mechanica mirifice compositum*) driven by water and showing the twelve hours which are sounded by an appropriate number of small bronze bells dropping into a brass basin. At noon twelve horsemen come out of twelve windows which close behind them'. Eginhard (*Annales*, ad annum) to whom we are grateful for this information added that 'there are many other things in this clock', and his words disclose the astonishment and the admiration that the Arabian clock aroused at the Frankish court. Nowhere in the West was it possible to make or to see such mechanical wonders. In A.D. 949, when Liudprand of Cremona visited Constantinople, he was admitted to the presence of the Greek emperor in a palace of remarkable size and beauty named Fresh Breeze. 'Before the Emperor's seat stood a tree, made of bronze gilded over, whose branches were filled with birds, also made of gilded bronze, which uttered different cries, each according to its varying species. The throne . . . was of immense size and was guarded by lions, made either of bronze or of wood covered over with gold, who beat the ground with their tails and gave a dreadful roar with open mouth and quivering tongue. Leaning upon the shoulders of two eunuchs I was brought into the emperor's presence. At my approach the lions began to roar and the birds to cry out . . . After I had three times made obeisance to the emperor with my face upon the ground, I lifted my head, and behold! the man whom just before I had seen sitting on a moderately elevated seat had now changed his raiment and was sitting on the level of the ceiling. How it was done I could not imagine, unless perhaps he was lifted up by some such sort of device as we use for raising the timbers of a wine press' (*Antapodosis*, VI, 5)[1]. Again the mechanical skill and ingenuity of the East caused wonder and admiration in an educated Western cleric.[2]

At the beginning of the thirteenth century there was still nothing in Western literature that could compare with Al-Jazari's technological encyclopaedia, composed about 1205 by this outstanding craftsman after twenty-five years spent at the court of the Urtuqid Sultan of Diar-Bekr on the Tigris.[3] The Byzantines of the thirteenth century did not find any reasons to modify those ideas to which they had been attached for centuries: namely that the 'Latins' (read Westerners) were just one kind of 'barbarians' and that the 'New Rome' (Constantinople) was so far superior to the Old that to compare the two would be ridiculous. Visiting distant China, Marco Polo felt like a 'barbarian' among more developed people. But the situation was rapidly changing. The sketch book of Villard de Honnecourt gives a significant indication of what was emerging in the West and two centuries later the technological preeminence of Western Europe over Asia was an accomplished fact. At the end of the fourteenth century, some Byzantines like Demetrius Cydones, taking a closer look at the Western culture, made the exhilarating discovery that the West had something to offer to the East.[4] Decades later, the Greek-born Cardinal Bessarion addressed to Constantine Palaeologos, despot of the autonomous Byzantine province of Morea, a memoir in which he spoke bluntly of Western superiority. In this memoir Bessarion urged Constantine to send young men to Italy.[1] These young men should 'learn the rudiments of some skills' and bring to Greece the more advanced Western technology especially in the fields of mechanical engineering, ship-building, the manufacture of arms and the iron industry.

'Mechanical engineering',—wrote the Cardinal—'facilitates the drawing of heavy objects, the demolition of ruins, the grinding of what needs grinding: boards are sawn auto-matically; mills turn as rapidly and exactly as possible; in metallurgy bellows are inflated and deflated without the touch of human hands, separating the metal from the baser material in the flux.

'The skill of making iron, so useful, so necessary to man-kind, the absence of which allows nothing to go smoothly whether in war or in man's peaceful political life, this too one might easily learn here at Rome. I hear that the Pelo-ponnese, and especially the district around Sparta, abounds in the ore of iron. Yet of all the necessities of life, Sparta lacks iron manufactures and must import them from elsewhere.

'The preparation and manufacture of armaments, both offensive and defensive, without which no war can be carried on satisfactorily, you can put into effect for yourself and the rest of Greece, especially if you have the iron in your country and acquire in addition those skilled in its manufacture.

'You ought naturally to value highly the art of ship-building also, since its benefits are most advantageous, and not only the building of warships and triremes, but also of merchant ships, the timber for which abounds in the Pelo-ponnese and is of the highest quality.

'These four skills ... mechanics, the manufacture of iron, the manufacture of arms and shipbuilding, necessary and useful as they are for those who wish to live well, you would be able to import into Greece and transfer to our people through the expedient of having four or eight young men introduced here (in Italy) in a suitable and unobtrusive way.

'Indeed, there are four other skills worthy of mention: the manufacture of glass, silk-weaving, the manufacture of woollen cloths and in addition the art of dyeing both. But since these are skills which were devised rather for luxury and amusement than for the sheer necessities of men, I lay little stress on these before the acquisition of the skills which are absolutely necessary'.

4—When the letter by Cardinal Bessarion was being written, Italy—or, more accurately, northern and central Italy—was undoubtedly one of the leading European countries in matters of craftsmanship and technology. That a humanist such as Cardinal Bessarion should choose Italy, the cradle of humanism, as the example to offer for the education and development of the young generations of his own country is perfectly justified and completely understandable. Italy, however, was not the only area in Europe to enjoy at that moment a developed technology and a relative abundance of craftsmen. The Low Countries, especially the southern Low Countries, were from this point of view no less developed than Italy. France, too, had plenty of skilled technicians. Her development had been hampered by the destruction and the disorder caused by the Hundred Years' War (1337-1453), but she recovered very rapidly and brilliantly in the second half of the fifteenth century. At almost the same time, thanks to the influences and impulses radiating from the Low Countries and from Italy, western and southern Germany experienced a remarkable development; by the end of the fifteenth century the Germans were masters in metallurgy and mining.[1]

The areas just mentioned were the cradles of late medieval and early Renaissance technology. On the fringe, other countries took part in a more or less passive way in the general European development, but by the standards prevailing in the Low Countries, in western and southern Germany, and in northern and central Italy they could easily be defined as underdeveloped. Spain had some nuclei of good craftsmanship in Biscay, Catalonia, and Toledo, but Catalonia entered a period of decline after the middle of the fourteenth century. In general, one could say with Guicciardini, at the beginning of the sixteenth century, that poverty prevailed in Spain 'not so much for the quality of the country, but because the Spaniards by nature are not inclined to the arts and crafts'.[2] The Scandinavian countries were no better off. England was in somewhat better shape; she had developed a fairly good textile industry and was the most advanced country on the periphery of Europe. However, she was far behind France, Germany, Italy and the Low Countries. In the first half of the sixteenth century she was still heavily borrowing craftsmen and techniques from the Continent for a number of trades, particularly mining and metal working.[3]

The basic asset of the more developed countries was their stock of human capital, namely their relatively large number of active merchants and good craftsmen. This capital was the result but at the same time also the cause of growth and development, and throughout the Middle Ages and the Renaissance rulers and administrators not only fussed over the imports and exports of foodstuffs and bullion: they were also deeply concerned about the inflow and outflow of craftsmen and the local supply of able artisans.

The mobility of skilled labour before the Industrial Revolution is a topic that has not been adequately investigated by economic historians and we know relatively little about it. There is no doubt, however, that the phenomenon existed on quite a large scale and that it was of great importance in the technological and economic history of Europe. I have already mentioned that skilled artisans often left their villages. Urban craftsmen were no less mobile. We often hear of master-artisans or groups of master-artisans who left one town for another or one country for another, fleeing from political troubles, from an epidemic, or from an economic crisis. 'Vagabundi sunt ut aves' was said of peasants in a medieval document, but the same thing could be said of craftsmen.

Religious fanaticism and a series of major European wars greatly fostered the mobility of labour in the course of the sixteenth century. Italy, which had attracted numerous foreign craftsmen throughout the previous centuries,[1] was the first to suffer from the political and religious upheavals of the sixteenth century. The Franco-Spanish Wars (1494-1559), with their tragic trail of famines, epidemics, and depression induced many skilled artisans to leave the country. This exodus tapered off somewhat in the second half of the sixteenth century but it resumed strength during the critical decades of the seventeenth century when the country's economy collapsed[2]. France profited from a large influx of Italian craftsmen during the first part of the sixteenth century but after 1560 she was torn apart by feuding religious and political groups and lost many skilled workers. In the southern Low Countries, Spanish conquest and occupation, Catholic fanaticism, and Dutch blockades proved disastrous: the whole economy collapsed in the course of the second half of the sixteenth century and capable craftsmen left the country in increasing numbers[1]. Germany supplied with skilful craftsmen the rest of Europe throughout the fifteenth, sixteenth and seventeenth centuries. It is impossible to give meaningful global figures about these movements and their directions, but we can say with a fair degree of plausibility that Italy, the southern Low Countries, France and Germany were on the whole the areas that lost precious human capital, while the Dutch United Provinces, England, Switzerland and, later, Sweden were the countries that profited correspondingly.

If the stimulus of skilled immigrants was to have lasting effects on an economy, the recipient country had to be open to new ideas and new techniques. Many Italian technicians went to Turkey in the course of the fifteenth and sixteenth centuries[2] yet nothing happened to the Turkish economy. On the other hand, the emigration of skilled artisans, while contributing to the decline of a country, was also a symptom of it. Italy, for instance, which lost many able craftsmen, had turned from a dynamic and highly receptive society into an obtusely conservative one in the course of the sixteenth and seventeenth centuries. The Italians, of the late Renaissance, wrote Fynes Moryson at the beginning of the seventeenth century, 'thincke themselves to have somuch understanding, and their Country to yealde somuch sweetenes, fruitfullness and such monuments of arts and fabricks, as they seldome or never travaile into forayne Kingdomes, but driven by some necessity ether to followe the warrs or to traffique abroad: this opinion that Italy doth afforde what can be seene or knowne in the world, makes them only have homebred wisdome and the prowde conceete of their owne witts . . .'[3]

As it happened, the countries which were receiving

skilled labour also adopted a new version of the Christian faith whose essential bibliolatry fostered the diffusion of literacy, thus contributing to the qualitative improvement of the stock of human resources. The combination of these and other factors played a decisive role in changing the balance of economic power in Europe between 1550 and 1650. Two centuries after Cardinal Bessarion urged the youth of his country to go to Italy to learn the best technology of the West, leadership in technological and economic development had been taken over by England, Holland, and, as far as metallurgy was concerned, Sweden.

5—In the meantime, important developments were taking place on the cultural level. The official seats of higher learning—the Universities—had remained relatively untouched by the cultural changes that the prevalence of merchants and craftsmen had brought about. The study of law, of course, was influenced by the development of trade, and theology had to come to terms with some of the needs of a commercialized society, but fundamentally the Universities remained strongly tied in their outlook to a distant past. The majority of medieval scholars scarcely recognized technological progress or showed any interest in it.

But the tide was turning with the rise of experimental science after the end of the Middle Ages. One can easily agree with Dr. R. Hall when he denies 'that the behaviour of an empirical scientist is derivable by virtually direct imitation from the trial-and-error, haphazard and fortuitous progress of the craft' and one can also agree with Dr. Hall's other statement that 'while scholars showed increasing readiness to make use of the information acquired by craftsmen and their special techniques for criticizing established ideas and

exploring phenomena afresh, it is far less clear that craftsmen were apt or equipped to criticize the theories and
procedures of science'[1]. But it would be a *non sequitur* to
argue that the social and technological environment of
the times played no role whatsoever in the intellectual
change among the learned. One must be careful to avoid
putting things in terms of a naive dichotomy in which
full-grown scientists face simple craftsmen[2]. History works
in a more subtle way and through a much more complicated network of channels. Before becoming a full-grown
scientist, a man must go through the state of childhood and
adolescence when he is influenced by what he sees and
hears in his family circle, among his friends and in the
street. Dr. Hall maintains that the spectacular achievements
of applied technology did not 'arrest the attention of
scholarly scientists'[3], but all that had been accomplished
with gunpowder, the magnetic compass, and the press
most certainly influenced the environment in which the
young men who were the scientists-to-be grew up and
were formed[4]. If people such as Francesco Di Giorgio and
Leonardo, who were above all and essentially artists,
delighted in drawing mills, gears and machines instead of
flowers, fishes and butterflies as their contemporary Chinese
fellow painters did, the explanation lies in those anonymous
but overpowering influences that the environment exerts
on men from their childhood on, in shaping their tastes
and their values. Similarly, if one pauses to consider the
utilitarianism and practicality that pervaded the outlook of
the new scientists[5], one can hardly help being reminded of
the effects of a social environment in which merchants, professionals and craftsmen had been for a long time the most
vigorous and dynamic group.

Although much about the origins of the Scientific
Revolution remains obscure, we know much about its

33

essence and its main aspects. An increasing number of scholars asked questions within the range of an experimental answer by limiting their enquiries to physical rather than metaphysical problems and by concentrating their attention on accurate observation of the kinds of things that are in the natural world. At the same time they accepted as a goal of science that subjection of the natural environment that has formerly seemed to belong only to art and the crafts. Their success was based on the combined application of measurement, mathematics, and experiment, and it was precisely those branches of science which were most amenable to measurement that showed the most spectacular achievements[1]. Resistance to change was not weak or easy to overcome. If there were passionate champions of the new science, there were no less passionate advocates of traditional scholarship. The conservatives clustered quite naturally around established institutions, namely the Universities. The champions of the new science founded new institutions, the Academies, and clustered around them.[2] In the long run, the innovators won. Their victory was the victory of a new philosophy imbued with empiricism and utilitarianism that infected all branches of human knowledge[3]. Mathematics was to be the main tool of analysis and the machine was the reference-idea. The whole 'management of this great machine of the world,' wrote H. Powers in 1664, 'can be explained only by the experimental and mechanical Philosophers'[4]. Indeed, what started then was the 'mechanisation of the world view'.

The utilitarian spirit, born of the medieval urban civilization, fostered by the humanism of the Renaissance and narrowed and emphasized by the Baconian philosophy, expressed itself in an ever-growing craze for new machines[5] and in an avid interest in those manual crafts that were responsible for the making of such contraptions. On the other hand, mechanics, chemistry, microscopy, qualitative astronomy were still in their infancy and there were no important barriers blocking entry into these new areas of exploration. Gabriel Harvey wrote in 1593 that any 'expert artisan or any sensible industrious practicioner, howsoever unlectured in schooles or unlettered in bookes' could make notable contributions to the advancement of science. This was a rosy overstatement. About a century later more realistically Evelyn complained in a letter to Boyle of the 'many subjections which I cannot support, of conversing with mechanical capricious persons'[1]. Nevertheless one can quote a number of cases in which ideas and suggestions were exchanged among scientists and highly-skilled crafts-men such as clockmakers, lens-cutters and precision-instrument makers. Professor Needham is essentially correct when, contrasting the European situation with the situation prevailing in China, he writes that: 'In Europe, unlike China, there was some influence at work . . . that pushed forward to make the junction between practical knowledge and mathematical formulations . . . Part of the story undoubtedly concerns the social changes in Europe which made the association of the gentleman and technician respectable'[2]. In fact a good part of the story concerns also the socio-cultural changes that made it respectable for the gentleman to apply himself to technical and scientific matters. Besides scholars and craftsmen there was in Europe a large and growing group of amateur-scientists who were neither professional scholars nor craftsmen. The role of these *virtuosi* in fostering the progress of science during the seventeenth and early eighteenth centuries can hardly be overstated and was certainly greater than that of the artisans.

The Chinese had invented the printing process many centuries before the Europeans discovered it, but it was the

Europeans who exploited it to the full. This is in fact a good case to illustrate the point that while an important technological innovation has a good chance to influence or modify the sociocultural environment, the ultimate effects of the same innovation rest on the nature and the quality of the environment. By the early seventeenth century, the great majority of the Chinese population was still illiterate while in Europe literacy had made remarkable progress. The large group of amateur-scientists who substantially contributed to the flourishing of Academies and to the progress of the Scientific Revolution would hardly have existed if literacy had been restricted to a few high priests and if printing had not developed into a flourishing industry.

As long as technological progress was mostly in the hands of common craftsmen who were guided mainly by tradition and some rough rules of trial-and-error, the rate of progress could never have been very high, but it accelerated dramatically when the resources of craftsmanship were strengthened by the systematic application of scientific principles developed by more or less professional scientists. It is enough to go through the records of patents issued in England, Holland, and France in the course of the seventeenth century to realize how important the change was. New machines, instruments for navigation and for measurement, barometers, thermometers, microscopes, telescopes, contraptions of all kinds and descriptions were invented, and developed. It was in this environment that von Guericke's pneumatic pump—the ancestor of the steam engine—was born. When all these developments are considered, it is not at all surprising that some decades later the Industrial Revolution took place—in fact, it would be highly surprising if it had not.

I THE EUROPEAN MASTERS

1—From the earliest antiquity, man has created various devices to solve the problem of the measurement of time. Sundials were the first solution and they continued to be widely used well into the sixteenth and seventeenth centuries, long after the appearance of mechanical clocks. Their low cost and their precision account for the great variety of types that were developed in the course of the centuries[1]. But the sun does not always shine, and man had to invent other instruments: water clocks and fire clocks[2] were developed in the ancient world; more recently, sand glasses came into use,[3] and in our atomic age they are still used for timing the boiling of eggs.

Of these different devices, the water clock or *clepsydra* seems to have been the one that offered to ingenious craftsmen the greatest opportunity for developing extravagant variations on the basic principle. The primitive form of water clock was a stone vessel from which the water was allowed to escape slowly through a small hole, time being indicated by the level of the water within. In the course of time more elaborate *clepsydrae* were made, containing mechanisms that moved automata and struck the hours[4]. It does not take an extreme flight of fancy to imagine that once *clepsydrae* with trains of wheels had been constructed, some craftsman must have thought of the desirability of sub-

stituting for the flow of water some other motive power.[1]
At the same time, there were craftsmen who were bothering
their heads with bells and all possible mechanisms for ringing
them effectively.

Bells played a prominent role in the life of medieval
towns: they ruled the life of the community and their
sound lifted 'all things unto a sphere of order and serenity'.
Everybody knew their meanings, and bells rang out their
messages at all times, telling the hours, announcing fire or
an approaching enemy, calling the people to arms or to
peaceful assemblies, telling them when to go to bed and
when to get out of it, when to go to work, when to pray
and when to fight, marking the opening and closing of
fairs, celebrating the elections of popes, the coronations of
kings, and victories in war. According to a widespread
belief, the sound of bells also helped to keep away storms
and epidemics. It was a matter of pride for a town, a
church, a monastery to have a beautiful bell or peal of bells,
and in the course of time, mechanisms were developed to
ring bells with greater efficiency: it is not improbable that
these contrivances, which were made of toothed wheels
and oscillating levers, helped to prepare for the development of mechanical clocks[2]. Finally, there were astronomers, astrologers and others interested in making globes
and spheres and in supplying them with movements that
would imitate the movements of the stars and the planets.
The historian is inclined to fancy that techniques developed
in the making of these devices must also have brought
craftsmen closer to the making of mechanical clocks[3].

If a broad historical point of view invites one to stress
the continuity and gradualness inherent in the process of
technological change, a strictly technological point of
view forces one to emphasize the fundamental difference
between water clocks, bell-ringing mechanisms, and the

like on the one hand and the mechanical clock on the other. Historians of technology and science have good cause to dramatize the sharp break in the history of horology brought about by the invention of the verge escapement with foliot. In the water clock, the time-keeping is governed by the rate of the flow of water through a hole, and the regulating device is simply the hole through which the water flows. In the mechanical clock, the time-keeping is governed by an oscillator or escapement which controls the unidirectional movement of the motive power and transforms it into a slow, steady and regular motion whose meaning appears on the face of the clock. The verge escapement with foliot is a most ingenious device and, as has been said, whoever invented it must have been a mechanical genius. The interested reader will find a technical description of the device below in the Appendix; here it suffices to say that the mechanical clock was born when the verge escapement with foliot was invented. Historians have long debated the dating of this invention but the general consensus now places it in the second half of the thirteenth century.[1]

Towns were then booming and the new urban civilization was asserting itself with unprecedented vigour, as yet unhampered by the rigidities that develop in the course of time around institutions, traditions, and vested interests. The thirteenth century saw the diffusion of the Universities and of the Gothic cathedrals, the aesthetic revolution brought about by Giotto and Cimabue, the voyages of the Polos to China and the first effort by Europeans to sail along the west coast of Africa, searching for a sea passage to the East; the second half of the century saw the making of the first cannon[2]. It was not entirely by chance that the mechanical clock and the cannon appeared at approximately the same time. Both were the product of a remarkable growth in the number and quality of metal workers, and as we shall see later, many of the early clockmakers were also gunfounders. The simultaneous appearance of the gun and the mechanical clock was both a testimony to the character of European development and a forecast of things to come.

It has recently been suggested that the mechanical clock had a Chinese origin, and those who favour this theory point to a remarkable piece of machinery built in China toward the end of the eleventh century. This contraption consisted essentially of a huge water mill that operated globes, spheres, and the like, and was equipped with some kind of escapement that timed the noisy movements of the whole thing. The Chinese escapement however had nothing in common with the European verge-and-foliot device. The suggestion therefore is that stories of the 'heavenly clockwork' must have reached Europe and 'perhaps . . . some scholar-craftsman puzzling over the tale that in the East they used a set of oscillating levers, tripping and holding back a wheel so to regulate its turning . . . made his own oscillatory device'[1]. Allowing their fancy an equally free rein, some Arab circles maintain that Dante's *Divine Comedy* was an imitation of the celestial fantasy written three centuries earlier by Abu'l-Ala al-Ma'arri.

In the course of the fourteenth century mechanical clocks became progressively more numerous in Europe[2], and very soon they were equipped with mechanisms for striking the hours. A clock made of iron was installed at the church of St. Eustorgio in Milan in 1309[3]. The cathedral at Beauvais had possibly a clock with a bell before 1324[4]. In 1335, according to an Italian chronicler[5], the church of St. Gothard in Milan had 'a wonderful clock, with a very large clapper which strikes a bell twenty-four times according to the twenty-four hours of the day and night and thus

'Horloge de Sapience' — miniature from a French manuscript, first half of the fifteenth century. On the picture, see the articles by Michel, *Horloge de Sapience* and Simoni, *Orologio a cembalo*

A clockmaker's shop — miniature from the manuscript *De Sphaera,* end of the fifteenth century

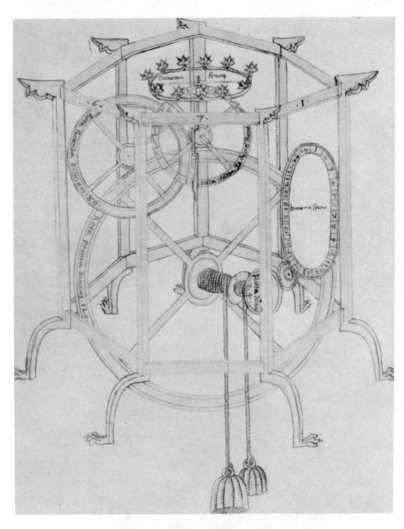

Copy of Giovanni Dondi's drawing of the mechanism
of his astronomical clock, Padua, 1364

Modern reconstruction of Dondi's clock in the
Smithsonian Institution

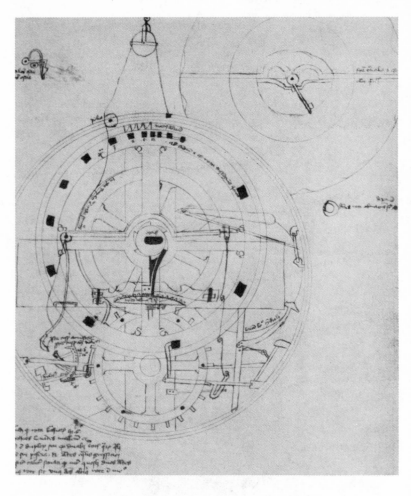

Design for a hanging clock driven by its own weight
probably by Jean Fusoris, c.1365-1436

at the first hour of the night gives one sound, at the second two strokes . . . and so distinguishes one hour from another which is of greatest use to men of every degree (*quod est summe necessarium pro omni statu hominum*)'. The monastery of Cluny had a clock in 1340 and by 1359 the Cathedral of Chartres had two[1]. In Padua a public clock that 'through days and nights tells the twenty-four hours automatically (*sponte sua*)' was installed in 1344. Public clocks that rang the hours appeared in Genoa for the first time in 1353, in Bologna in 1356 and in Ferrara in 1362[2]. In 1370 Charles V of France installed a clock that struck the hours on one of the towers of the royal palace[3], and so pleased was he with this that he had similar clocks installed at the Château de Vincennes and the Hôtel Saint-Paul. Being afraid that their sound could not be heard by everyone in town, he also ordered all the churches in Paris to ring their bells '*par pointz à maniere d'orologe*' when the royal clocks struck the hours. Thus everyone could know the time '*luise le soleil ou non*'[4].

A clock, especially a big public clock, was very expensive in those days. It was expensive to build[5], and its maintenance, which generally included the regular wage of a specially appointed 'governor'[6] was a severe drain on local finances. The decision to install or not to install a clock was often the result of long and heated debates, but it appears that in general people took great pride in their public clocks[7] and considered them essentially useful things. The Milanese chronicler was convinced that the clock in the church of St. Gothard 'was of greatest use to men of every degree'. Having in mind the clock installed by Charles V on the Royal Palace in Paris, Froissart wrote:

> L'orloge est, au vrai considerer
> un instrument très bel et très notable
> et s'est aussi plaisant et pourfitable

car nuit et jour les heures nous aprent,
par la soubtilleté qu'elle comprent
en l'absense meïsme dou soleil
dont on doit mieuls prisier son appareil[1]

In 1473, Bartolomeo Manfredi asserted that the complicated cosmological indications of the public clock in Mantua (Italy), served the purpose of showing 'the proper time for phlebotomy, for surgery, for making dresses, for tilling the soil, for undertaking journeys and for other things very useful in this world'[2]. In 1481 a petition presented to the Town Council of Lyon stressed the fact that in the town 'is sorely felt the need for a great clock whose strokes could be heard by all citizens in all parts of the town. If such a clock were to be made, more merchants would come to the fairs, the citizens would be very consoled, cheerful and happy and would live a more orderly life, and the town would gain in decoration'[3]. In an age in which nobody, or very few, had a portable clock, the usefulness of the public clock striking the hours was unquestionable; but practicality was not always the only motivation. Some towns rivalled others for the distinction of having, as a fifteenth-century French document put it, '*relotgium magnum sufficiens et honorabile ad honorem villae*'[4]. About 1380, the Town Council of Lyon decided to install on one of the bridges a tower with a clock similar to one on a bridge in Paris: '*prout et quemadmodum edificate sunt Parisiis turris et horologium desuper existens*'[5]. In the 1420's the Town Council of Romans (France) decided to build a very beautiful clock 'without any regard to expenses' ('*sans regarder à la depense*'). In 1557 the inhabitants of Montélimar (France) decided to have a clock similar to that of Romans: '*a la forme d'icelluy de Romans*'[6].

Thus a combination of civic pride, utilitarianism, and

mechanical interest fostered the diffusion of the clock despite its relatively high cost. Since more clocks were being made, the proficiency of the makers improved, and by the end of the fourteenth century, clocks which struck the hours and the quarters had been built[1], but this fact should not mislead us regarding the precision of these early time-keepers. As has been said, early clocks 'embodied a strange combination of brilliance in conception with a deficient technique of construction'. Throughout the fourteenth and fifteenth centuries, most clocks (if and when they worked), lost or gained much time in a day, and on the other hand, contemporary requirements for precision were low: thus it was generally thought unnecessary to provide clocks with a minute hand. In 1389 the city of Rouen granted a stipend to the wife of a clockmaker for turning the clock two or three times a week; in all likelihood, she had to reset the hand to correct the time[2]. In 1387, King John of Aragon decided to employ two men to strike the bells of the clock in his castle of Perpignan since the clock itself failed to strike correctly[3]. The people of Paris referred to the clock of the royal palace in the following rhyme: '*l'horloge du palais, elle vas comme il lui plait.*' There is no doubt that until at least the sixteenth century even the best clocks kept the time only roughly and had to be reset by sundials once in a while. As late as 1641 the town council in Dijon, noticing in desperation that no one of the public clocks agreed with the others, gave the peremptory order that they should be put in accordance '*suivant le cours du soleil*'[4].

The most striking occurrence in the early history of clocks is that while medieval craftsmen did not improve noticeably in precision, they soon succeeded in constructing clocks with curious and very complicated movements. It was easier to add wheels to wheels than to find better ways to regulate the escapement. On the other hand complicated movements had quite a popular appeal and most people believed that a correct knowledge of the conjunction of the heavenly bodies was essential for the success of human enterprises. One of the most remarkable pieces in this regard was the clock made about 1350 for the cathedral of Strasbourg. Enormous in size, it included a moving calendar and an astrolabe whose pointers indicated the movements of the sun, moon and planets. The upper compartment was adorned with a statue of the Virgin before whom at noon the Three Magi bowed while a carillon played a tune. On top of the whole thing stood an enormous cock which, at the end of the procession of the Magi, opened its beak, thrust forth its tongue, crowed and flapped its wings[1]. In Bologna around the middle of the fifteenth century Master Giovanni Evangelista da Piacenza and Master Bartolomeo di Gnudolo built an impressive clock on the *Palazzo del Comune*, with a trumpeting angel, a large number of Saints and other holy dignitaries and a procession of the Magi who payed their respects to the Virgin and Child. The most remarkable thing, however, was the astronomical section of the clock. Built under the supervision of that great humanist, Cardinal Bessarion, the astronomical section allegedly showed 'a central globe of fire around which the sun, the moon, the earth, the planets and the skies rotated harmoniously'[2]. This arrangement was based on the cosmological views held by the disciples of Pythagoras and it was in open contrast with the Ptolemaic theories prevailing in the fifteenth century. The famous clocks of Orvieto and Reggio in Italy, of Wells in England, of Lund in Sweden, of Lübeck in Germany, and of Berne in Switzerland were not quite as impressive as the clock of Strasbourg or so unorthodox as the clock of Bologna but they were, none the less, extraordinary pieces[3]. For the sake of beauty and civic pride, complicated movements were sometimes added to existing clocks. This was done in Parma (Italy) in 1431 and the chronicler, obviously class-conscious, wrote that the new contrivances told the hours 'to the commoners' ('*al popolo*') and the position of the moon to 'those who can understand' ('*agli intelligenti*')[1]. In 1510 an elaborate jack-work was fitted in the clock on the belfry of Ghent (Flanders): a man (Adam) struck the hours, a woman (Eve) struck the half-hours and a snake moved around obviously trying to induce Adam and Eve to indulge in other and more synchronized kinds of movements. The masterpiece of the Middle Ages, however, was the astronomical clock made about 1350 by Giovanni de' Dondi, probably with the help of his father Jacopo. It was only incidentally a timepiece: as a matter of fact it was more remarkable for its astronomical work than for its actual clockwork. It included the celestial wanderings of sun, moon, and five planets and provided a complete and perpetual calendar. Philippe de Maizières, who saw and admired it, described it as follows: 'There is in Italy today a man exceptionally versed in philosophy, medicine and astronomy who is by general consensus recognized as the greatest living authority in these three sciences. His name is master John de Dons and he lives in the city of Padua. Because of his great knowledge in astronomical matters his family name is generally forgotten and he is called master John of the clocks. He is now with the Count of Virtú[2] and he gets a salary of two thousand gold florins a year for his knowledge in the three fields. This master John of the clocks has produced famous works in the three sciences, works that are held in great repute by the great scholars in Italy, Germany and Hungary. Among other things, he has made an instrument, called by some a sphere or clock for the celestial movements; which instrument shows all the movements of the signs and the planets with their circles and epicycles, and differences, and each planet is shown separately with its own movement in such a way that at any moment of the day or of the night one can see in which sign and to which degree the planets and the great stars appear in the sky. The sphere is constructed in such a subtle way that in spite of the fact that there are so many wheels that they cannot be counted without taking the clock to pieces, all goes with one weight. So great is the marvel that great astronomers come from distant places to admire his work. . . . In order to have his sphere done as he had it in his subtle mind, the said master John actually forged it with his own hands out of brass and copper, without the help of anyone, and he did nothing else for sixteen years'[1]. The masterpiece was eventually placed in the library of the Visconti castle at Pavia, but after the death of John of the clocks, nobody knew how to take care of it[2]. Nowadays the admiration for the horological masterpiece of Master John has not yet subsided. The clock was destroyed in the course of time, but we know its mechanism thanks to an accurate description made by Master John himself and handed down to posterity[3]. Alan H. Lloyd, an expert in such matters, thinks that 'had a similar clock been devised and made today in spite of all the knowledge and machinery that would be available to the maker, he would be regarded as an outstanding man'[4], and Professor L. White adds: '(Giovanni's) sense of the interrelation of moving parts showed genius: to provide for the eliptical orbits of the Moon and Mercury (as required by the Ptolemaic system) he produced eliptical gears and likewise made provision for the observed irregularities in the orbit of Venus. In complexity and refinement Giovanni's gearing goes enormously beyond anything which survives from earlier technology, including the fragments of the Hellenistic planetarium found in the Aegean Sea. In this aspect of machine design, the fourteenth century marks an epoch'[1].

2—Most of the clocks mentioned in the previous pages were public clocks. Since mechanical time-keepers were very expensive, it is only natural that their early diffusion should be greater in the public sector where the necessary funds could be raised through voluntary or compulsory joint financial effort[2]. Domestic clocks, however, were not completely lacking. When that extraordinary collector of *objets d'art* Charles V of France died in 1380, the officials who made the inventory of the 3,985 items of his collection found among them 'one clock all made of silver and with no iron, that had belonged to the late King Philip the Fair, with two weights covered with silver and filled with lead'[3]. This must have been a domestic clock driven by weights and it must have been constructed before 1314, the year of Philip the Fair's death. The 'sphere' constructed by Dondi no matter how exceptional for its astronomical intricacies, was also essentially a domestic clock. Other examples of domestic and portable clocks can be found if we search the dust of the archives[4], but it can be said with a good deal of plausibility that they were extremely rare until the middle of the fifteenth century. For one thing, they cost too much; for another, a clock was considered to be a very intricate, delicate, and unpredictable machine which required the continual care of a 'governor' who had to 'rule, set, guide and keep it'. Even Charles V, who had more than one clock in his collection of *objets d'art* and who had installed public clocks in some of his palaces, relied on specially graduated candles to measure the time in his own room. Domestic clocks, said Christine de Pisan to whom we are grateful for the information, '*encore n'estoyent communs*'[1].

Yet the diffusion of public *horologia*, which had made people accustomed to clocks, paved the way for the diffusion of domestic clocks. After the first craze for the big and elaborate public *horologia* had subsided, one has the impression that more time and ingenuity were devoted to the making of smaller, portable pieces. The forces of the market were slowly but irresistibly indicating that it was in this direction that production could in the course of time find larger outlets.

As long as weights were the only motive power, house clocks were not easily movable; they had to stand on brackets or be spiked to the wall. In order to construct easily portable clocks, a new kind of motive power had to be devised. According to a contemporary of Filippo Brunelleschi, the great Italian architect was very interested in clockwork and by 1410 was constructing clocks driven by 'various and diverse kinds of springs'[2]. The word that the Italian biographer used, '*molle*', undoubtedly means 'springs' but one cannot say that his description sounds very technical. On the basis of this passage alone, one would hesitate to conclude that by 1410 spring-driven clocks had appeared in addition to weight-driven ones. However, a French miniature dating from about 1440-1450 portrays in great detail the mechanism of a portable clock that was spring-driven[3]. The same miniature and other and earlier documents illustrate an ingenious device, the fusee, which had the function of preserving a more or less constant torque throughout the running time of the spring. Available evidence seems therefore to indicate that the use of the spring in timepieces dates back at least to the first decades of the fifteenth century[4]. The importance of the invention can hardly be overestimated, for it made possible the construction of easily portable clocks and, later, the construction of the watch.

Throughout the second half of the fifteenth century, domestic weight-driven clocks were still very rare and spring-driven clocks even more so.   About 1450, an important personage of the Burgundian court who owned a spring-driven clock had it painted in the background of his portrait[1]. In 1481 King Louis XI of France paid £16 10s. (*tournois* money) 'to Jehan of Paris, clockmaker, for a clock that has a dial and strikes the hours, complete in all its parts; which clock the King bought to carry with him in all places where he shall go'[2]. That the king was very proud of this piece is clearly indicated by the fact that he too had it painted in one of his portraits[3].

It was in the sixteenth century that domestic clocks and watches became much less of a rarity[4]. If one compares the European scene with other parts of the globe during the sixteenth and seventeenth centuries, one is impressed by the fact that there were many more craftsmen and merchants in relation to total population in Europe than elsewhere. But no less striking and no less important was the fact that in Europe between the few who were very rich and the many who were very poor there existed a relatively large group of urban dwellers—merchants, lawyers, notaries, doctors, apothecaries and the like—who could afford decent houses, good clothes, and a few amenities of life. The two facts, one acting on the side of supply and the other on the side of demand, were firmly interlocked: each one existed only because of the other. In sixteenth and seventeenth century Europe there were not only craftsmen who could make timepieces but also a relatively large number of people who could buy them. Thus the production of clocks and watches progressively expanded.

49

What had happened previously to the public weight-driven clocks happened in a more or less similar way to spring-driven portable clocks and watches: after their first appearance, craftsmen spent most of their time and effort in constructing pieces with complicated calendrical and astronomical movements or in devising curious shapes[1]. As far as precision is concerned, clocks and watches remained relatively poor time-keepers throughout the sixteenth century and the first half of the seventeenth. Of course, some progress was made[2]: in the course of the sixteenth century the minute hand appeared more frequently, and one can find in museums some outstanding clocks of that period that keep time with a remarkable degree of accuracy[3]. One may recall, for instance, the clocks made by Jost Burgi and by Jost Bodeker. However one should not generalize from a few exceptional specimens and assume these museum-pieces to be a representative sample of the norm. The invention of new and better escapements and the solution of some difficult problems of applied mechanics were necessary in order to make possible the large scale production of ordinary time-keepers possessing a satisfactory degree of precision.

3—In the fourteenth and fifteenth centuries the demand for clocks was not great enough to allow for the growth of a specialized group of craftsmen. The earliest clockmakers were mostly blacksmiths or locksmiths or gunfounders; in other words, they were craftsmen who knew how to work metals and who on occasion also managed to produce or to repair mechanical time-keepers. At the beginning of the fifteenth century, Jacques Yolens of Lille was 'a clockmaker and a gunner'[4] and master Pierre Cudrifin of Fribourg was '*magister bombardarum et horologiorum*'[5]. In the Genoese colony at Caffa (Crimea) in 1455 Ubaldinus de Florentia was '*bombarderius et magister orologii Comunis*'[1]. Henricho, the parson who was appointed governor of the clock at the Church of St. Gothard in Milan in 1474 was a reputed expert in matters of bombards[2]. After the end of the fifteenth century Noël Cusin, governor of the clock of the cathedral of Autun, made clocks, organs, and cannon[3] and in Lisbon Master John, probably from Germany, was a gunner and a clockmaker[4]. Other examples can easily be found in great numbers[5]. This colourful type of versatile craftsman actually survived for a long time in those places where the manufacture of timepieces did not develop into an important economic activity. In Flensborg (Denmark) in the 1550's Gert Merfelden made cannon and clocks and in the first part of the seventeenth century in Randers (Denmark) a craftsman made clocks and shafts for carriages[6]. In Dundee (Scotland) in the 1580's, a Patrick Ramsay who 'did thankful service by his good attention on the knok and steeple' of St. Mary's Church was 'smith and gunmaker'[7]. In seventeenth century Basel (Switzerland) 'locksmith and clockmaker' was a common professional qualification[8] and as late as the 1730's most of the craftsmen who repaired clocks and watches in Berlin were 'locksmiths[9]'.

In the areas of medieval Europe where metal workers were scarce and the mechanically-inclined ones were rare, clocks were often constructed by foreign craftsmen. In Catalonia most of the clockmakers were Jews[10]. In fourteenth century England the clocks of the cathedrals of Salisbury and Wells were in all likelihood made by foreign craftsmen brought to England by Bishop Erghum, himself a foreigner[11]. In 1368 Edward III granted protection and safe conduct for one year to John Vueman, William Vueman and John Lietuyt of Delft (Holland), 'orlogiers coming into the Realm to practice their art'[12]. When foreigners were not at hand, friars occasionally devoted themselves to the task. In England Father Richard of Wallingford is credited with the construction of horological devices in the early part of the fourteenth century[1]. In the 1360's a clock was made for the Pope in Avignon by a friar from Venice[2]. In fifteenth century Sweden, some friars of the Vadstena monastery were interested in horology and the astronomical clock in the Dome at Uppsala was made in 1507 by one of them[3]. In 1537 the town clock at Aberdeen (Scotland) 'was reformed and mended by friar Alexander Lyndsay'[4].

Germany (using the geopolitical term in its wide medieval connotation)[5] appears to have had a relative abundance of capable smith-clockmakers: the German craftsmen very early acquired a good reputation and were often invited to countries such as France and Italy where native craftsmen were not lacking. In 1370, when Charles V of France wanted to install a public clock in his palace, he brought to Paris a German craftsman, Henry de Vic; in 1407 it was another German, Jehan d'Alemaigne, 'locksmith' who made in Paris 'a small clock (*petite orloge*) to be put in the room of the Queen'[6]. In the fifteenth century, some German clockmakers were working in Milan, Rome and other Italian towns[7]. However, although skilled smith-clockmakers were more numerous in some areas than in others, there were no real centres of clock-making in Europe until the end of the fifteenth century. Clocks were usually produced where they were consumed, and it was the craftsmen who travelled, not the merchandise[8]. Clockmakers were in demand because there were few of them[9], but they could hardly settle in numbers in any one place because the local demand for their work was easily saturated. For all these reasons, as well as for the fact that they were hardly distinguishable from other metal workers, the clockmakers had no guild of their own. Thus to the very end of the Middle Ages the organization of the craft retained certain primitive features long since abandoned by the textile industry and other trades.

In the course of the sixteenth and seventeenth centuries the greater demand for domestic clocks and watches permitted the formation of settled groups of artisans. First, Augsburg and Nuremberg emerged as centres of clockmaking. Later on, other centres developed such as Blois, Paris, Lyon, Geneva and London. In Paris there were about twenty master clockmakers beside an unknown number of workers and apprentices at the middle of the sixteenth century[1] and about seventy masters in the 1640's[2]. In Blois there were about seventeen masters in 1600 and about forty-five in 1639[3]. In Lyon there were more than ten masters in 1570, about sixteen in 1610, and between forty and sixty just after the middle of the seventeenth century[4]. In Geneva there were more than twenty clockmakers toward the end of the sixteenth century[5] and their number grew very rapidly in the following decades[6]. In Augsburg in 1615, there were forty-three master clockmakers beside forty-three journeymen who had come to Augsburg from other towns and had not yet been granted citizenship[7]. In London there were probably more than sixty masters in the 1620's[8]. In some of the centres where they grew in numbers and in wealth, the clockmakers eventually established their own guild—in Paris in 1544, in Blois in 1597, in Geneva in 1601, in Toulouse in 1608, in London in 1631, in Lyon in 1658-60, in The Hague in 1688, in Stockholm in 1695, in Copenhagen in 1755[9]. These cases should not be generalized. In many a town, the clockmakers never had their own guild and instead belonged to the guild of the smiths[10]. In many other towns there was scarcely a clockmaker until very recent times[11]. Interestingly enough, Italy, which had been a leading country in matters of horology during the Middle Ages, did not develop any great centre of clock and watch-making in the modern age[1]. Outstanding clockmakers were not completely lacking and skilful craftsmen were often invited from France and Germany by Italian princes[2]. But in the course of the sixteenth and seventeenth centuries the country underwent a drastic process of social involution which was concomitant in the seventeenth century with a process of commercial and industrial decline[3]. Thus the situation that eventually prevailed in Italy was one of a few outstanding craftsmen who worked mostly under the patronage of Princes, Popes and other dignitaries producing artistic pieces for aristocratic circles[4].

As long as most of the clocks were huge public timekeepers made of iron or bronze it is perfectly understandable that their makers were smiths, locksmiths, gunsmiths, and metal workers in general, but the situation changed in the course of the sixteenth and seventeenth centuries when domestic clocks and watches became less of a rarity. The smaller timepieces were expensive contrivances and were owned by well-to-do people. Being luxury items they were at the very centre of the craze for exuberant decoration that characterized the late Renaissance and the Baroque Age[5]. The craftsmen who had to satisfy the new vogue now needed the skills of the goldsmiths[6] rather than those of the blacksmiths and locksmiths. In England, France, Germany, Italy and many other places a clear-cut distinction developed between 'makers of big public clocks' and 'makers of little clocks and watches'[7]. The materials used by the 'makers of little clocks and watches' were often expensive and for those who specialized in the production of highly ornate clocks and watches the necessary investment in working capital was quite substantial[8]. Masters with a rich clientele or princely patrons enjoyed good economic conditions[1]. In those centres like Geneva where, as we shall see, clockmaking developed into a prominent industry, clockmakers also acquired a prominent social position[2]. In general, however, clockmakers were not wealthy people and clockmaking was not considered an especially rewarding profession[3]. A French document of the 1580's ranking for fiscal purposes the professions practised in Paris in five classes according to their estimated economic worth, put clockmaking in the third class[4]. In the Netherlands, in the late seventeenth and early eighteenth centuries, professions were ranked in four classes and clock and watchmaking was put in the second class[5]. These broad generalizations probably did not err on the side of optimism[6].

Who were the clockmakers and what was their social origin? John de' Dondi, the scholar, was a special case, although not a rare one[7], and the same can be said for the friars who turned clockmakers[8]. After the middle of the fifteenth century, at least in the more developed areas, the great majority of clockmakers came from the large social stratum of artisans that was a characteristic of European towns. Of thirty-three clockmakers who worked in Lyon in the period from 1550 to 1650 (and whose fathers' professions we know) thirteen were sons of clockmakers and two each were sons of goldsmiths, merchants, teachers and tailors. Of the remaining twelve, one was the son of an apothecary, one of a surgeon, one of a shoemaker, one of a metal-founder, one of a gunsmith, one of a mint master, one of a lace worker, one of a proxy, one of a carpenter, one of a clerk, one of a constable, and one of an unskilled labourer. In Blois (France), among clockmakers and apprentices who worked there from 1550 to 1700, more than sixty-five were sons of clockmakers, four were sons of merchants, three each were sons of goldsmiths and carpenters, two were sons of surgeons, one was the son of an apothecary, one of a clerk, one of a notary, one of an architect, one of a gunsmith, one of an armourer, one of a tailor, one of a locksmith, one of a constable and one of a tax collector[1]. Other examples that can be collected from other areas confirm this picture. An apprentice clockmaker in Geneva in 1569 was the son of a gunsmith, another in 1672 was the son of a professor of philosophy and a third one in 1674 was the son of a doctor[2]. In England Thomas Tompion was the son of a blacksmith, John Harrison was the son of a carpenter, Thomas Mudge was the son of a clergyman and John Arnold was the son of a watchmaker[3]. Jacob Deburges, who was born in England and moved to Blois in the 1590's, was the son of a bookseller[4]. In seventeenth-century Basel two apprentices were sons of clockmakers and one was the son of a deacon[5]. In those places where guilds of clockmakers were established, the corporative system obviously influenced the social structure of these local groups of clockmakers. For one thing, it emphasized and institutionalized the distinction between masters and labourers[6]; for another, with the establishment of high and differentiated fees for apprenticeship or for acceptance into the guild, it restricted the area from which the masters could be drawn[7] and it strengthened the tendency to make the profession hereditary within certain families[8].

As a rule, medieval scholars were not interested in machines, but the clock, because of its connection with astronomy, was an exception. Mention has already been made of the contributions to horology by medieval friars and by the two Dondis, both '*philosophie, medicine et astrologie doctores*' at the University of Padua. In the Renaissance, while clocks and watches were becoming progressively more fashionable in the upper classes as useful and graceful ornaments, the clock as a machine attracted more and more the inquisitive curiosity of scholars, amateur scholars and learned people in general. According to Vasari, Brunelleschi 'together with some studious persons, looked into the matter of time and of movements, of weights and wheels, and how to make them work and he himself made some very good and very beautiful clocks'[1]. Lorenzo della Volpaia was '*eccellentissimo maestro d'oriuoli et ottimo astrologo*' and built a very elaborate public clock for Lorenzo il Magnifico[2]. The great Leonardo was interested in clockwork and he actually depicted in one of his sketches a kind of escapement that seems to indicate that he had some idea of using the pendulum as a time-regulator. In the sixteenth century two famous mathematicians Chretien Herlin and Conrad Dasypodius worked at the great clock of Strasbourg Cathedral[3].

In the seventeenth century, when the Scientific Revolution exploded in all its exuberance and vigour, the champions of the new science manifested an avid interest in horological matters. In their eyes the clock was the machine *par excellence* and it fascinated them. But there was more to it than that. The sixteenth and seventeenth centuries witnessed the great astronomical discoveries and the great expansion of ocean navigation: both astronomers and navigators needed precision time-keepers to determine longitude and the right ascension of the stars[4]. At the same time, the construction of high-precision time-keepers presupposed the solution of basic problems of mechanics that were at the very heart of the Scientific Revolution. Among those who devoted themselves to the problems of measuring time and of constructing accurate clocks one can mention Galileo, Christian Huygens, Robert Hooke, Godefroy Wendelin, Nicolas Fatio, and Wilhelm Leibniz[5].

Until the middle of the sixteenth century the verge escapement with foliot remained unchallenged and the construction of all time-keepers depended on that rather crude device. In the course of the seventeenth century, however, when scientists devoted their attention to the problem of the measurement of time, they applied scientific principles and systematic experimentation to horology. Scientists and clockmakers then worked in close collaboration[1] and the result was a series of revolutionary discoveries and a break-through in the technological progress of the craft. The most important step was the introduction of a new mechanism which used the pendulum instead of the foliot as the controlling device. Galileo had had in mind a solution of this sort, but it was Christian Huygens who solved the problem in the late 1650's and inaugurated the production of pendulum clocks.

The importance of the innovation is shown in the graph opposite. For the period preceding 1800, the values represented in the graph are of course only rough estimates of the average accuracy of the best clocks of the time[2], but with all their limitations the data are sufficiently revealing to indicate the importance of Huygens' discoveries. The appearance of the pendulum ended the era of the low-precision time-keepers and opened the era of the high-precision instruments. On a more general level, the graph shows the dramatic discontinuity in the history of technology that took place in the course of the seventeenth century, which abundantly justifies the expression 'Scientific Revolution'. The progress in applied technology that followed that 'Revolution' appears to be of exponential kind. In the narrow field of horology a series of important discoveries and innovations accompanied and followed the birth of the pendulum clock, but all that was happening in horology was but one aspect of a broad and complex set of interlocking technological changes. Clockmaking was the first industry to put into practice the theoretical findings of physics and mechanics. At the same time, it set the pace for the general development of applied mechanics and played a role of prime importance in the evolution of scientific instruments. As has been written, 'the earliest achievements in precision mechanics, and the essential steps in its progress up to the present day, must be credited to horology. . . . At a very early date clockmakers devised tools with which the most delicate operations of their trade could be accurately performed . . . they were led to investigate the properties of the types of copper and steel used in their work, to study the thermal expansion of metals, the elasticity and resilience of springs. They invented and per-

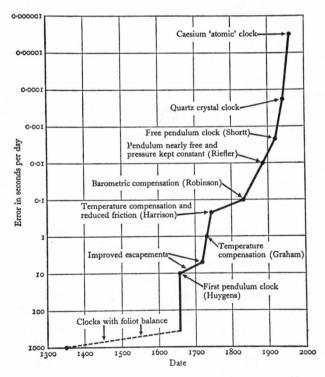

fected machines for the manufacture of some of their simpler tools.

'Thus, apart from strictly horological inventions, thanks to which the precision of timepieces was continually improved, the clockmakers placed at the service of the science of mechanics an array of equipment which was constantly being perfected and had only to be taken over, directly or indirectly, by the constructors of instruments'[1]. It was not by chance that the century that witnessed the appearance of the first accurate timepieces was also the century that witnessed the birth of the industry of scientific precision instruments in general[2]. '*Les instruments précis font progresser la science, tandis que la science permet l'amelioration des instruments précis*': after a long period of gestation, our modern scientific age was born—and cumulative processes progressively accelerated its further development. Lewis Mumford overstates the case when he writes that 'the clock, not the steam engine, is the key machine of the modern industrial world', but his hyperbolism contains more than a grain of truth.

4—In 1745, referring to the export of English clocks, J. Cary wrote that 'we sell little but art and labour, the material whereof clocks are made being but of small value'[3]. In 1843, in an evaluation of costs in the production of watches in Geneva, J. A. Bloch Borel estimated that the raw materials (gold and silver) accounted for about two-sevenths of the cost and labour for about five-sevenths[4]. It may well be that in the sixteenth and seventeenth centuries the ratio on the average was somewhat more favourable to the raw materials input, but even for those centuries one can hardly over-estimate the relative importance of labour. It must also be noted that the raw materials used in the construction of chamber clocks and watches were of light weight and small volume and could easily be transported over long distances at a reasonable relative cost, even in an age when transport was far from easy. Thus the availability of raw materials played only a small role in the geographical location of the industry. Two other factors seem to have been far more important: the demand for timepieces and the supply of skilled labour. The growth of the clockmaking industry in Blois and Paris was undeniably related to the demand of the court, the aristocrats, and the rich bourgeois for clocks and watches. In other places it was a combination of local demand and commercial organization that captured foreign demand and transmitted its stimuli. Demand was a necessary factor but it alone was not sufficient to account for the growth of clockmaking in certain areas; the supply of skilled labour must also be taken into consideration.

I have already mentioned that there were no centres of clock manufacturing worthy of the name until the end of the fifteenth century. Toward the end of the century, however, Augsburg and Nuremberg developed into such centres[1]. In the course of the middle ages, both towns had developed a great tradition in metal-working. Moreover, the two towns were great commercial centres that offered good opportunities for exports. The combination of these circumstances allowed clockmaking to grow and prosper.

By the beginning of the sixteenth century, the Nuremberg and Augsburg masters and their products were known all over Europe. Their fame became so great that Peter Henlein of Nuremberg, was for a long time incorrectly credited with the invention of the watch[2]. We have no information about the number of clockmakers in Nuremberg. For Augsburg three censuses of 1610, 1615, and 1619 indicate that there were about forty master-clockmakers and an almost equally large number of workmen in the town[1].

The period of brilliant economic growth seems to have come to an end toward the middle of the sixteenth century but in matters of horology the fame of the two German towns lasted well into the first decade of the seventeenth century. Still at the end of the sixteenth century, time-pieces made in Augsburg and Nuremberg were being exported to distant foreign markets[2], and the Italian Garzoni wrote that 'a great number of German craftsmen excel in the art of horology and all the best and the most precise timekeepers actually come from Germany'[3] Circa 1600 Fynes Moryson wrote that 'tuching manuall arts, the Dutch are a people more industrious then the Germans and excell them in all arts and trades . . . howsoever I must confesse that the Germans of Nurenberg in those parts are esteemed the best workmen for clockes and some like thinges'[4]. This supremacy was brought to an end by the decline of some of Nuremberg's and Augsburg's traditional customers such as Italy in the South and Antwerp in the North as well as by the havoc of the Thirty Years' War (1618-1648). In Augsburg, according to a census, only seven master clockmakers were left in town in 1645[5].

Clockmakers had many traits in common with the other craftsmen of their age: with few exceptions they were violent and riotous in their youth, litigious in their adult years, and dishonest whenever the occasion arose[6]. Among them there were, of course, the illiterate as well as the literate ones, but on the whole clockmakers were dis-tinguished among other craftsmen for a relatively high degree of literacy[7]. In point of fact, a number of clock-makers were educated far beyond the level of reading and writing. Julien Coudray and Guillaume Coudray, clock-makers of Blois in the second half of the sixteenth century, frequented the Royal Library. Christopher Piron, who died in Blois in 1637, left in his estate 'une quantité de livres d'astrologie' and Jacques Duduict, who worked there in the early 1600's, was a good writer. Master Jehan Flanc, 'horlogeur de la Ville,' who died in La Rochelle in 1616, was 'sçavant aux mathématiques et aux fortifications'[1]. Clockmaking required certain skills in drawing and it was essential for clockmakers to be able to count[2]. In a number of contracts of apprenticeship made in Geneva in the course of the seventeenth century it was expressly stated that the master had 'to teach the apprentice how to read and write, and this especially in the first year of the apprenticeship'[3].

The Reformation apparently made a relatively large number of converts among the clockmakers. Of ninety master clockmakers who lived in Catholic Lyon during the period 1550-1650, and whose religion we know, fifty were Catholic and forty were Protestant. We had no precise figures for Paris but some evidence seems to indicate that the situation there was similar to the one existing in Lyon. Information about clockmakers who turned Protestant is also available for other places such as Blois, and La Rochelle[4]. It is reasonable to suppose that there was some connection between the high degree of literacy prevailing among clockmakers and their relatively high propensity to follow the Reformation movement. Whatever the reasons for their religious inclinations, the clockmakers were often persecuted in the southern Low Countries, France and Italy, and thus one encounters them frequently in the history of those migrations of skilled labour that helped to change the balance of economic power in Europe.

Here in fact lies one of the fascinating aspects of the social history of horology in those days: until at least the end of the seventeenth century the industry did not need great capital equipment[1] or an elaborate organization; given satisfactory conditions on the side of demand, a handful of craftsmen was all that was needed to make a great centre of production. As I have already indicated, there were less than two dozen master clockmakers in Paris in the middle of the sixteenth century, and the masters who made Lyon a centre of the clock industry were no more numerous. To destroy or to build up the industry it was enough to dismiss or to attract a dozen craftsmen. We, today, are not so vulnerable at the level of horology, but at higher levels the selective massacre of a dozen scientists would bring more than one branch of science to a standstill. While Nuremberg and Augsburg declined, Geneva and London emerged as major centres of clockmaking. In both places the development of the industry was related to the inflow of a handful of refugees[2]—to the injection of a small but precious amount of human skills.

In 1449 there was one clockmaker in Geneva[3]. In the tax-list of 1464 no clockmaker is mentioned[4]. In 1515 when the clock of the church of St. Pierre got out of order, there was no craftsman in town who could repair it. Shortly after 1550, a few clockmakers began to arrive in Geneva as refugees: Philippe Bon and a Master Bayard came from Lorraine, a Master Somellier from Dieppe, Laurent Drondelle from Paris, Pierre Charpentier from Orleans, Pierre de Fobier from Languedoc. The list could continue: in it one would find clockmakers from the Southern Low Countries, from Italy, from Germany, but mostly from France. Geneva's gates at that time were open to all who were escaping from religious persecution; it was actually in Calvin's interest to increase the number of his adherents after he had defeated the party of the Libertines. The immigration does not seem to have caused economic difficulties. On the contrary, the rapid growth

Two sixteenth century engravings of clockmakers' shops

Frontispiece of a seventeenth-century horological
work published in Italy

of the working population was accompanied by a remarkable economic renaissance, partly because the immigrants were mostly skilled craftsmen[1] and partly because Geneva was traditionally a commercial centre with fairs that offered excellent opportunities for exporting. The ensuing prosperity also brought to Geneva people who, as a contemporary document disapprovingly mentions, were attracted more by the opportunity of 'practising their craft than by the Gospel'. Clockmakers were not very numerous among the refugees[2] but as I have said before a handful of craftsmen was all that was needed in those days to make a centre of clock manufacture; on the other hand, those few clockmakers proliferated rapidly. About 1600 there were in Geneva twenty-five to thirty master clockmakers and an unknown number of workmen and apprentices[3]. By the 1680's there were, according to Gregorio Leti, more than one hundred masters and about three hundred workers who produced more than 5,000 timepieces a year[4].

London's story is not unlike that of Geneva. During the reigns of Henry VIII and Elizabeth I, a fairly large number of foreigners were allowed to settle in England. Often the immigrants aroused the hostility of English craftsmen and the May Day riot of the London Apprentices in 1517 against the 'Stranger Artificers' shows to what degree of frustration the English craftsmen were driven by alien competition. At times also the legislation seems to have been calculated to deter rather than to encourage the advent of foreign artisans[5]. However, the aliens were successfully drawn into the industrial system of the country. On the other hand, the reaction of English craftsmen should not be misinterpreted. It did not signify lack of receptiveness to foreign ideas and technologies: it sprang from a widespread jealousy of foreign artisans[6]. 'English', wrote Fynes Moryson, 'prefer strangers as well phisitians as other like professors

65

then their owne countrymen as more learned and skillful then they are, which makes the English also so much travayle in forrayne parts and so much esteeme theire owne countrymen being travelers'[1].

In *Hedda Gabler*, when Ibsen wanted to show Hedda's husband as a dull and pedantic man, he mentioned that the husband was at work on a study of the textile industry in the sixteenth century. My opinion of scholars concerned with the sixteenth century textile industry is a more charitable one, but I suspect that in recent times excessive concern with the stagnation of export of English woollens after 1550[2] has dulled our view of English economic and social history in Elizabethan times. Some scholarly circles have devoted much time and brilliant energies to prove that there was no Industrial Revolution before the Industrial Revolution. One can easily agree with this unexhilarating view, yet one can still submit that in Elizabethan England innovation was the strikingly predominant note in many basic fields such as education, shipbuilding, navigation, overseas trade, the building trades, and the iron industry not to mention the 'quantitative' approach by which some of these activities were being analyzed for the first time.

In matters of horology English backwardness was conspicuous until the last decades of the sixteenth century. When Henry VIII wanted to have some work done on the clock at Nonsuch Palace he had to import French clockmakers to do it[3]. Nicholas Cratzer 'deviser of the King's horloges' was a Bavarian[4]. As for the production of watches, there is no record of an English watch before 1580 and only a short time before this date is there a record of a watchmaker[5]. But before the century was over signs of improvement and change were abundantly clear. The demand for timepieces was growing and foreign craftsmen were flowing into the country. Nicholas Urseau, clock-maker to Queen Elizabeth, was of French origin[1]. François Nawe who was producing clocks and watches in London in the 1580's[2] must also have been French to judge from his name. Their example was not lost, because Elizabethan Englishmen were conspicuous for some of the qualities that we nowadays associate with the Japanese. The first watches made by English craftsmen in the last two decades of the sixteenth century were unimaginative but diligent replicas of French and German models. A watch made by Bartholomew Newsam, appointed clockmaker to Queen Elizabeth in 1572 in succession to Nicholas Urseau, has a pierced cover of the German type. The striking watch made by Randolf Bull of London (now in the Mallet collection of the Ashmolean Museum at Oxford) is a good example of the composite type. The mechanism is French, the case is German, and the inner ring of hours from 13 to 24 on the dial is suitable for a system of counting time which was used in Germany but not in England[3]. In some cases English makers used for their watch and clock movements continental-made cases, which displayed a far finer quality and richness of design than any of English make[4].

Although they were willing to imitate foreign products, English clockmakers were not at all happy about the unre-mitting immigration of foreign artisans. In 1622 the 'Clockmakers Citizens and inhabitants in London' angrily complained to the Crown that they were 'interrupted and discredited in the use of their trade by the interposition of manie straingers invadinge this Realme', and of course they accused the 'straingers' of all sorts of 'abuses'[5]. Five years later the 'Free Clockmakers of the City, complained again of being 'exceedingly oppressed by intrusion of clockmakers strangers' and especially by 'the Ffrench

clockmakers'[1]. According to a list of names attached to
the document of 1622 there were sixteen English clockmakers 'householders' in London and about thirty 'knowne
straingers of ye same arte dwelling in and about London'
as well as a certain number of foreign apprentices. The
names of the 'straingers of ye same arte' indicate in most
cases a French origin. Although most of the French
masters were Huguenots, a few were not. In *A True
Certificat of the Names of the Straungers residing and dwellinge
within the City of London* taken by the Privy Council in
1618, one finds in the ward of Farrington within, a 'Bernaby
Martinot, clock-maker, born in Paris, a Roman Catho-
lique' and in Portsoken Ward a 'John Goddard, clockmaker, . . . a papist'[2]. Incidentally, in the list of 1622 one
finds a Lewis Cuper who had emigrated to London sometime between 1613 and 1622[3]. The Cupers were at that
time a famous family of clockmakers in Blois, but the
family was of German extraction and had settled in Blois
sometime before the middle of the sixteenth century[4]:
in this roundabout way skills and technologies were
broadcast throughout Europe.

There are reasons to suspect that the list of 1622
maliciously underestimated the number of English clockmakers[5], but even if we were to double the number
declared, the resulting ratio between 'English' clockmakers
and 'straingers' would still prove that in London as in
Geneva the most relevant factor in the growth and development of the clock and watchmaking industry was the
immigration of foreign craftsmen.

As late as 1657 England was still borrowing from the
Continent in horological matters: in that year John
Fromanteel, a member of a family of Dutch extraction
that had settled in England in the early part of the century,
went to Holland to learn the art of making pendulum

clocks of the type recently invented by Huygens and made by Coster; on John's return the Fromanteels were the first to make pendulum clocks in England[1]. However, in the course of the seventeenth century English makers made noticeable progress, establishing original lines of thought and acquiring an undisputed supremacy over their continental colleagues. With men of inventive genius such as the famous Dr. Hooke (1635-1703), they improved the precision of timekeepers and invented a number of ingenious horological devices. Among such devices one should mention the anchor escapement that appeared around 1670. This escapement had the advantage of greatly reduced wear. Furthermore it enabled the use of a long pendulum with a small arc without recourse to intermediate gearing thus allowing for more precise measurement of time. One should also mention the repeating mechanism. In an age when the lighting of a house was not a simple matter, telling time was a difficult problem at night. In France M. de Villayer allegedly solved the problem by designing a clock with a dial that had different kinds of spices inserted in the place of numbers. At night he reached for the point indicated by the hour hand and tastefully determined the time[2]. English clockmakers searched for less gastronomical solutions and in the 1680's Daniel Quare and Edward Barlow produced repeating devices for watches and clocks[3].

By 1680 England had attained an unchallenged preeminence in the field of horology. At the same time an unmistakably English style emerged in the form and decoration of case work: so typically and unmistakably English that it was found unpalatable in France[4].

5—By the dawn of the eighteenth century, London and

Geneva were by far the two greatest centres of clock and watchmaking in Europe[1]. With the emergence of these two centres, new proto-industrial and proto-capitalistic ways of doing things appeared in the trade and in the making of timepieces. Especially after the first half of the seventeenth century, specialization developed among craftsmen in the more advanced clockmaking centres with regard to the production of single parts of timepieces. The spring makers were apparently the first specialized workers to appear[2], but other specialists soon followed[3]: at the beginning of the eighteenth century many streets in Clerkenwell, a district of London, were occupied by workmen who were escapement-makers, engine-turners, fusee-cutters, secret-springers, and finishers[4]. As early as 1701 the making of a watch was chosen to illustrate the advantages of division of labour[5]. In Geneva two groups of specialized workers succeeded in having a guild of their own, distinct from the guild of clockmakers: thus the assemblers had their guild recognized in 1698 and the chiselers in 1716[6]. Quite naturally these developments affected trade also: one reads only of clocks and watches being traded and sold before 1600, but after that date there are frequent references to transactions concerning single parts of clockwork[7]. At the same time, the changed conditions caused the actual craftsman to become divorced from the retail side of the business.

The corporative structure with its distinction among masters, labourers and apprentices remained in existence but above these three categories a new group emerged, numerically small but economically powerful. This was the group of the clock merchants, proto-capitalistic entrepreneurs who placed orders with the masters, advanced funds to them, and arranged for the marketing of the merchandise at home or abroad. This particular type of organization seems to have developed more fully in Geneva[8].

These developments came to full maturity in the course of the eighteenth century and resulted in the mass production[1] of common and relatively inexpensive timepieces. Savary noted that Geneva exported 'some excellent timepieces, but a much greater quantity of common ones'[2]. Adam Smith wrote that 'the diminution of price has, in the course of the present (eighteenth) and preceding century, been most remarkable in those manufactures of which the materials are the coarser metals. A better movement of a watch, that about the middle of the last (seventeenth) century could have been bought for twenty pounds, may now perhaps be had for twenty shillings'[3]. At the same time technological progress made possible further substantial improvements in the precision of timepieces (see graph I, p. 59).. The reverse of the coin, the price paid for greater efficiency on both the economic and technological planes, was more vulgarity and cheapness on the artistic level[4]. The mass produced timepiece with interchangeable parts, and made by specialized workers, was leading the way toward the Industrial Revolution[5].

Much of what was happening on the side of production was interlocked with what was happening on the side of demand, namely the growth of a steadily rising proportion of middle-class and relatively prosperous people who could afford to buy timepieces. The combination of developments both on the side of demand and on the side of supply resulted in a greater diffusion of clocks and watches[6] and Savary could write that 'horology . . . has become one of the most active and advantageous branches of the trade'[7]. It is not surprising therefore that in a number of countries more attention was devoted to this 'branch of trade'.

The idea of developing a clock and watch industry appealed to the tastes and inclinations of the enlightened rulers as well as of the enlightened philosophers and scientists of the eighteenth century. In the second half of the century the King of Prussia repeatedly tried to establish a manufacture of timepieces in Berlin. A similar attempt was made by the Margrave of Baden in 1767. A pilot factory for the production of watches and clocks was established at Dubrovno in Bielo-Russia in 1784, and in 1792 it was moved to Kupavno, near Moscow. About the same time the King of Portugal established a clock factory in Lisbon. The engineer and inventor Pohlem had a factory operating at Stjernsund, in Dalecarlia (Sweden) at the beginning of the eighteenth century; and Voltaire set up a manufacture at Ferney (France) in the 1770's[1]. These and other initiatives met with different fates: a few of them succeeded, most of them failed. The most interesting and lasting developments anyhow occurred in Paris.

As has been indicated in previous paragraphs, Paris was one of the first towns to emerge in Europe as a centre of the clockmaking industry. Political troubles and religious strife possibly hampered the development of the industry in the second half of the sixteenth century[2], but although we lack precise information, there are reasons to believe that in the first half of the seventeenth century the industry was still expanding. In 1646 the clockmakers felt the need to limit to a maximum of 72 the number of masters admitted to the guild[3] and this decision may reasonably be assumed to indicate that the number of clockmakers in Paris was growing. From the middle of the seventeenth century, however, the situation deteriorated. The guild regulations hampered development and opposed innovation while the competition of Geneva grew progressively stronger. Amidst these troubles, the Edict of Nantes was repealed. There is no doubt that the economic effects of the Revocation have been occasionally exaggerated[4], but it would be difficult to maintain that what happened in

1685 and in the following years did not damage the clock industry. Professor Scoville has proved that the Huguenots who left France were a very small proportion of the total active population and he deduces from this that the consequences of the emigration cannot have been of great relevance[1]. The argument is sound as far as it goes but it does not go very far: it may hold for those branches of the economy in which large numbers of craftsmen were available, but horology was a field in which, as we have already seen, a small number of craftsmen could make quite a difference[2]. Whatever their relative weight, the combination of restrictive guild regimentation, foreign competition and emigration of rare and skilled human resources proved highly disruptive. At the beginning of the eighteenth century, an official paper reported on the bad conditions of the French clock and watch industry and pointed out that it was impossible to have a timepiece in France that did not contain parts imported from London or Geneva[3]. It was at that juncture that the French administration took steps to improve the conditions of the industry

History works often through curious ways. As has been indicated above, London largely owed the development of her horological industry to the immigration of French craftsmen. At the beginning of the eighteenth century, in order to revitalize the French industry, the French administration invited to Paris an English clockmaker of great repute, Henry Sully, and with him sixty other English craftsmen. The establishments set up by Sully at Versailles and at St. Germain did not take firm root and disappeared within a few years; but, as the French themselves recognized, although the venture proved a failure, it nevertheless introduced to French masters a standard of workmanship superior to anything they had previously known. The products of Sully '*excitèrent l'émulation parmi les Horlogers de Paris*[1] and led to great advances in French horology, principally under the leadership of Julien Le Roy.

The progress of the industry was not an easy one: it was harassed by the unremitting competition of the Swiss manufactures. Low cost products from Geneva flooded the French market and there was nothing that the Swiss would not do to push their products. The Swiss clockmakers did not sign their clockwork so that on occasion they could sell them to other manufacturers who would then mark them with their own signature[2]; if London-made parts were requested, then the Swiss did not hesitate to imprint the mark of London on their own products[3]. In Paris, according to the brothers Castel, clockmakers in Bourg-en-Bresse, through some kind of bribery the Swiss managed 'to keep stocks of watches and clockwork in the Abbey of St. Germain and other privileged places supplying many a clockmaker with their products'[4]. 'The Swiss watch industry ruins our manufactures', sadly remarked Beliard just after the middle of the eighteenth century[5] and the brothers Castel added that 'because of this trade of time-pieces from Geneva a considerable amount of money flows out of this kingdom every year'[6].

Yet these and other difficulties did not prevent the recovery of the French manufactures. The economic history of France in the two centuries 1550 to 1750 is an intriguing puzzle to the economic and social historian. To the distant observer the country seems always on the verge of a final collapse and all the odds seem to be against any possible recovery. Yet as the legendary phoenix, consumed in fire by her own acts, France always managed to rise in youthful freshness from her own ashes. An incredible amount of robust human energies must have been constantly fermenting under the troubled surface. In the narrow field of horology there is no doubt that after the first quarter of the eighteenth century the industry grew steadily and before the century was over, Paris was with London and Geneva one of the three main centres of the clock and watch industry in the world. By the 1770's an Italian author wrote that 'English craftsmen acquired great repute in Europe for the beauty and the precision of their products . . . but nowadays the clockmakers of Paris excel the English for the beauty and the neatness of their work'[1]. In the 1780's there were in Paris possibly more than 400 master clockmakers[2]. French watches were sold in London[3]. However until the end of the century, a more efficient commercial organization greatly favoured the products of London and Geneva, which largely prevailed on the international market[4]. Toward the end of the eighteenth century London produced a yearly average of about eighty thousand timepieces for export and about fifty thousand timepieces for the home trade[5]. Geneva possibly produced an average of seventy or eighty thousand pieces, which were, of course, almost all exported[6]. After the peace treaty of 1477, Mehmet II had asked Venice to send him a clockmaker. At the time only a few in Turkey knew of the existence of mechanical clocks. But in the course of time the taste for European clocks seeped down from the Court to larger strata of the Turkish society, while in the West, as shown above, the Italians and the South-Germans lost their leadership in horology to the English and the Swiss. At the end of the eighteenth century the products from England and Switzerland dominated the Turkish market, and as James Dallaway recorded, "English watches prepared for the Levant market are one of the first articles of luxury that a Turk purchases"[7].

By then English and Swiss timepieces were popular not only in the Middle East but also in distant China.

II CHINESE MANDARINS AND THE SELF-RINGING BELL

1—'A cynic might observe that if it was Christians and spices which had brought the Portuguese to the Orient, it was the spices which were instrumental in keeping them there'[1]. This remark by Professor C. R. Boxer is applicable as well to the motivations that brought and kept overseas the Spaniards, the Dutch, the English, the Danes, and the Swedes. Missionaries apart, Europeans went to the East solely to trade and until the end of the eighteenth century they were sensible enough to realize that overseas territorial conquests were not within the realm of reasonable possibility. Whatever conquests they attempted were, with a few exceptions, limited to islands and harbours to be used as entrepôts for their trading activities. Knowing that their technological and military superiority resided in their gun-carrying, ocean-going sailing ships, the Europeans were satisfied for almost three centuries to limit their control to the high seas[2].

When they first reached the Far East, Europeans were chiefly interested in spices but it did not take them very long to realize that a number of other commodities offered excellent opportunities for profit, e.g., copper from Japan, cotton textiles from India, silk and carpets from Persia, silk and porcelain and (after the end of the seventeenth century) tea from China. The chief obstacle to trade, however, was

76

the fact that they had almost no goods to offer in exchange for eastern products. Since the Industrial Revolution, we have come to take western superiority in the arts and sciences so much for granted that it is difficult for us to imagine a situation in which the East had much to offer in raw materials and manufactured goods while the West had very little that appealed to the peoples of Asia. Yet this was precisely the situation which prevailed throughout the sixteenth, seventeenth, and eighteenth centuries.

The gun-carrying, ocean-going sailing ship allowed the Europeans to establish themselves as the masters of the high seas, to destroy most of the Moslem shipping and trade, and to capture a large share of the intra-Asian trade. By bringing Japanese silver to China, Japanese copper to China and India, Spice Islands' cloves to India and China, Indian cotton textiles to South-east Asia, and Persian carpets to India, the Europeans made satisfactory profits and the income derived from their shipping and commercial services paid for some of the Asian products imported into Europe. But the income was not enough and by far the greater part of Asian imports had to be paid for by a massive transfer of bullion from Europe to Asia. Large amounts of silver in the form of *reales* or pieces of eight minted in Seville, Mexican dollars, silver coins minted in Italy and Germany, French crowns and Dutch rixdollars passed every year into Asian hands. Silver was abundantly available to the Europeans, thanks to the favourable balance of trade between Europe and the Americas. Leaving aside the relatively limited trade that was carried directly via the Philippines between the Spanish colonies of the Americas and the Far East[1], one can justifiably say that world trade at this time consisted essentially of a large stream of silver that moved eastward from the Americas to Europe and from there to Asia and of a large flow of commodities that moved in the opposite direction: Asian products went to Europe and European products went to the Americas.

The gap in the balance of trade between Europe and Asia was conspicuous even in a physical sense. People like van Linschoten observed that when the Indiamen 'go out they are but lightly laden, onely with certaine pipes of wine and oyle, and some small quantitie of merchandie, other things they have not in, but balast and victuals for the company, for that the most and greatest ware that is commonly sent into India are rials of eight'[1]. At the end of the sixteenth century a Florentine merchant reported that Portugal and Spain alone brought into China 'every year more than 1,500,000 escudos'[2]. How reliable this estimate is no one can say, but more accurate and more abundant figures are available for the seventeenth and eighteenth centuries and they consistently show that silver was the chief European export to Asia[3].

This situation caused much concern in Europe and produced heated debates as well as numerous publications on the subject. In both England and France the companies that carried the East Indies trade were violently attacked and accused of putting their own selfish interests over and above the public interest, of thriving at the expense of national power and wealth[4]. On a more practical level, unremitting attempts were made to improve upon the situation. In England the government required that at least one-tenth of the cargo of each Indiaman should consist of goods which were 'the growth, produce or manufacture of the Kingdome'[5]. The East India Company explored every conceivable opportunity 'to introduce (itself) into the trade of the citty of Nankin' and other cities in northern China, hoping that the cold climate would favour 'a considerable vent for our woollen manufactures'[1]. However, all these efforts ended in failure. European merchants even explored the possibility of exporting paintings and *objets d'art*, but western art was intensely concerned with religious subjects and, as Richard Cocke wrote from Japan, the Asian peoples were not interested in Biblical scenes. 'They esteem a painted sheet of paper with a horse, ship or a bird more than they do such rich picture. Neither will any one give six pence for that fair picture of the conversion of St. Paul.' After having tried without success to sell engravings of Madonnas and other religious scenes, the Amsterdam Company tried to sell prints that had 'a more general human appeal, a collection of nudes and less decent illustrations'[2], but these imaginative efforts also failed to achieve appreciable results. About 1701 the Council of the East India Company wrote to the court in London: 'We cannot tell what to advise your Honours to send to these parts (China), the natives being fond of nothing but silver and lead; and probably if the rest of your goods were thrown over board at sea, your cargo home would not be much less'[3].

The lack of eastern demand for western products was a serious problem, but even more alarming was the fact that Asian manufactures competed successfully with European products in the European market in important sectors of the economy. As J. Cary, a merchant of Bristol, put it, 'the East India trade I take to be very prejudicial to us, as 'tis not driven, because it exports our bullion, spends little of our product or manufactures and brings in commodities perfectly manufactured which hinder the consumption of our own'[4]. The story of the East India silks and calicoes that were imported into England and caused difficulty for the English textile industry is so well known that it does not need to be told here. It was fortunate for England that no Indian Ricardo arose to convince the English people that, according to the law of comparative costs, it would be advantageous for them to turn into shepherds and to import from India all the textiles that were needed. Instead, England passed a series of acts designed to prevent importation of Indian textiles and some 'good results' were achieved[1].

Similar feelings and reactions arose in France in connection with the importation of silk and textiles from China by the French East India Company. Interestingly enough, Colbert, the great 'mercantilist', did not assent to the petitions of the French producers who solicited protective measures, but his immediate successors did, and from 1686 onward a sequence of acts repeatedly forbade all imports of Asian textiles into France[2]. In 1717 and 1718 also Spain passed a law prohibiting the import of silk textiles from Asia[3].

2—As I have said, most of the European manufactures either did not interest the peoples of Asia or could not compete with similar products of Oriental making; but there were a very few exceptions and the mechanical clock was one of them.

As Father Matteo Ricci wrote, the timepieces used in China were 'made to operate by the means of water or fire, and in those which are operated by fire, time is measured by odoriferous ashes of a standard size. Besides the Chinese make also other clocks with wheels that are made to turn with sand. But all such instruments are very inaccurate. Of sundials, they have only the equinoctial ones but do not know well how to adjust them for the position (i.e. latitude) in which they are placed'[4].

Rumours of mechanical clocks reached Chinese circles

This portrait (c.1550) by Titian of an unknown Knight of the Order of Malta is a good example of the contemporary interest in clocks

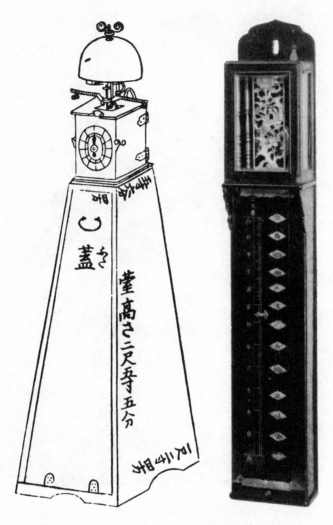

Left, a drawing of a pyramid clock from a Japanese book published in 1796; right, a Japanese pillar clock with both interchangeable scales and moveable numerals for the unequal hours (height 19¾ inches)

from Macao. The idea of 'self-ringing bells' (自 鳴 金童)
intrigued the Chinese immensely and the Jesuits seized
upon this interest as an opportunity for sneaking into
China. As Father Ricci himself relates the story, in 1582
'a native of the Province of Fukien, named Chen Jui was
Viceroy of Kwantung and Kwangsi; he was a capable
man and fond of money'. The Jesuits of Macao approached
him tactfully and let him know that they wanted to present
him with some gifts, including 'a clock that strikes the hours
automatically, a very beautiful object such as has never
been seen before in China'. Thus the Fathers went to the
Viceroy and 'presented him with the clock, a Venetian
triangular-shaped glass which shows the delights of various
colours and some other things. The Viceroy was extremely
pleased with the gifts and assigned the Fathers a residence
in a temple of idols called Tien nim tse, not far away from
his palace. There the Fathers received visits from some of
the Magistrates and other prominent citizens . . . and there
they lived for four or five months'[1]. They were beginning
to hope that the concession might develop into a permanent
grant when discouraging difficulties unexpectedly arose.
For some reason the Viceroy was relieved of his office;
realizing that the presence of the Jesuits in the city might
not be pleasing to his successor and might actually be the
object of an investigation, he requested the Fathers to with-
draw. After a month of 'great tribulations' the Jesuits were
back in Macao, filled 'with great sadness', but scarcely a
week had passed since their return to the island when they
were reached by a messenger of the governor of the district
of Schiaochin. With the authorization of the new viceroy,
the governor invited the Fathers to return to Schiaochin
and to take over a piece of property granted by the state
for the construction of a house. 'In order that the appearance
of a new religion might not arouse suspicion among the

Chinese people, the Fathers did not speak openly about religious matters. They spent their time courteously receiving visitors, in studying the language of the country, the methods of writing and the customs of the people. They taught by virtue of their example what they did not preach. They wore the outer garment of the prominent persons of the country: a long robe with very ample sleeves and this impressed the Chinese people very favourably'[1].

Always willing to oblige, the Fathers took advantage of every opportunity to be as helpful and as generous as possible. In December, 1583, one of them had to return to Macao to obtain financial help for the mission from the European community. The governor of Schiaochin let the Fathers know that he would dearly love to have one of the 'self-ringing bells' sold in Macao and that he was ready to pay whatever was necessary for it. The Jesuits were unable to find a clock for sale in Macao but they did find an Indian blacksmith 'of very dark complexion' who had learned from the Europeans how to make clocks. This blacksmith was brought to Schiaochin in lieu of the clock, a proof of good will which very obviously impressed the governor. Two of the best smiths in town were assigned to assist the visiting clockmaker and after a great deal of trouble a clock was eventually produced at the mission for Governor Wang Phan[2].

Clocks were also instrumental in opening the gates of the Imperial Palace at Peking to the Jesuits. As the story goes, the Jesuits petitioned to pay a respectful visit to the imperial court and to present the emperor with two clocks and some other gifts. One of the clocks was a large iron piece, driven by weights and richly ornamented with gilded dragons, eagles, and other figures; the other was a small spring-driven piece made of gilded bronze. Both were equipped with striking mechanisms[1].

Suspicious bureaucrats and malicious eunuchs caused all kinds of difficulties for the missionaries. At one point, in the middle of winter, Father Ricci and his companions found themselves prisoners in a fortress, and while the probability of their reaching Peking looked very tenuous indeed the probability of their being executed grew at an alarming rate. Yet at the very moment when there seemed to be no more room for reasonable hopes, events unexpectedly took a turn for the better. The Fathers were convinced that Divine Providence had come to their assistance 'in answer to the prayers of the many who were everywhere storming Heaven for the success of the expedition'. This was the age when in the West the universe was regarded as a great piece of clockwork and God as an outstanding clockmaker; perhaps this is the reason why Providence chose clocks to change the course of the events[2]. But let Father Ricci recount the story[3]:

'One day the King of his own prompting suddenly remembered having seen a petition by some foreigners who wanted to present him with a self-ringing bell. Thus he cried, "How is it that those foreigners do not give me the self-ringing bell?" The eunuch who always accompanies the King, replied, "If Your Majesty does not endorse the record, how would the foreigners dare come to the Court with no licence?" Whereupon the King endorsed the record and summoned the foreigners . . . The Fathers arrived in Peking at the end of the Chinese year, namely on the 24th day of January 1601. On their arrival they took up residence at the palace of the eunuchs, just outside the gate, and here they arranged the presents and made a list of them. The following day the presents were brought to the Imperial Palace with considerable show and excitement.

... The big clock, however, was not set and did not strike the hours, thus the King gave orders to summon the Fathers. This was done and they came post haste. . . . The Fathers were admitted to the second wall in a courtyard where the big clock had been laid and where a multitude of people had gathered. The King sent one of his high-ranking eunuchs named Li Chin who received the Fathers very graciously. He asked the Fathers many questions and he wanted to know their purpose in bringing presents to the King. He was quite pleased to know that they were not asking for any position and that they were religious people who served God with no interest in worldly goods. He was told that the clocks served to tell the time by day and by night, either by the striking of the bells or by the hands on the dials. The Fathers also explained that the clocks had to be regulated and that in two or three days they could give anyone the necessary instructions. The eunuch reported all this to the King and the King appointed to the task four eunuchs from the College of the Mathematicians which is within the Palace and is composed of twenty or thirty eunuchs. The four eunuchs had to learn how to regulate the clocks and to bring them into the King's room within three days. Thus the Fathers were lodged for three days in the quarters of the mathematicians and they spent days and nights teaching the four mathematicians how to take care of the clocks. They were always treated with great respect and the eunuch Mathan and his group paid for everything. It had been rumoured that he had accepted many valuable presents from the Fathers, which was not true, but Mathan had to disburse much money to silence the eunuchs who are close to the King.

'The four mathematicians learned very diligently everything pertinent to the clocks. They actually wrote down everything they were told for they could not afford to forget any detail since this could cost them their lives. The King is so cruel to them that even for a slight fault the poor unfortunates are beaten to death or killed in some other manner. Their first care was to ask for the names in Chinese of all wheels, pinions, keys, and every other part of the clocks, and this the Fathers did, creating names both in the spoken and in the written language. . . . The three days assigned for instruction had not passed before the King called for the clocks. They were hastily taken to him and he was so pleased with them that he promoted the four eunuchs to a higher rank, which is a way to give them more authority and more income. The eunuchs were delighted, especially because, from that day on, two of them were permitted to enter the presence of the King to wind the small clock which he always kept with him day and night. . . .

'There was no place in the Imperial Palace where the big clock could be set to allow the weights to fall low enough to govern the wheels. So in the following year the King sent the clock to the Department of Public Works and gave the order to build a suitable wooden tower according to the design made by the Fathers. This tower had staircases, windows, and balconies, and it is very beautiful indeed. He also had the bell of the clock replaced by a new one. The clock tower was indeed worthy of royalty and one thousand and three hundred ducats were spent on it. By royal order the clock tower was placed outside the second wall of the Palace, in one of the gardens of the King, where he often goes for recreation and where he keeps many other precious things'.

The passion of the Sons of Heaven for the 'self-ringing bells' never faded away. Throughout the seventeenth and eighteenth centuries clocks, automata, and similar devices of great beauty and ingenuity flowed unceasingly into the Imperial Palace in Peking. Emperor K'ang Hsi (1662-1722) went so far as to set up a workshop for the manufacture of clocks and watches in the Palace[1] and the Jesuits, with characteristic pliancy, recruited professional clockmakers into their ranks and incorporated them into the China Mission. In 1707 an accomplished Swiss clockmaker, Father Stadlin[2], was dispatched to Peking to assist in the establishment and operating of the imperial workshop and until the suppression of the Jesuit Mission, there was always a Jesuit in charge of the emperor's clock collection and factory. In the 1730's Father Valentin Chalier[3] wrote: 'The Imperial Palace is stuffed with clocks . . . watches, carillons, repeaters, organs, spheres and astronomical clocks of all kind and description—there are more than four thousand pieces from the best masters of Paris and London very many of which I have had through my hands for repairs or cleaning. I must know as much of the theory now as any clockmaker in Europe, for I am sure few have had as much experience'[4]. According to Father Chalier, about one hundred Chinese worked under him during his superintendency of both the collection and the factory in the 1730's and 1740's[5].

Emperor K'ang Hsi was filled with admiration, rare in his dynasty, for the arts and sciences of Europe, but even the emperors who had no sympathy for the West or leanings toward Western technology never allowed their feelings to interfere with the preservation and enrichment of the fabulous imperial collection. Simon Harcourt Smith studied the remains of the collection after its despoilment on the sack of Yuan-Ming Yen in 1860 and the Forbidden City in 1900 and its further destruction in the troubles of the early decades of the twentieth century. Even then he was able to reconstruct sufficient evidence to write that 'in the Imperial Palaces at Peking, Yuan-Ming Yen and Jehol the passage of the hours was marked by a fluttering of enamelled wings, a gushing of glass fountains and a spinning of paste stars, while from a thousand concealed and whirring orchestras the gavottes and minuets of London rose strangely into the Chinese air'[1].

3—The interest in the 'self-ringing bells' was not confined to the upper circles of Chinese society; the populace too never failed to manifest great wonder and admiration when they viewed the new contrivance. At the Jesuits' House in Schiaochin, Father Ricci and his companions installed a public clock that struck the hours and unfailingly attracted a large number of curious idlers to the mission[2]. Similarly in Peking the drum-operated carillons built by the Jesuits produced exhilarating effects on the populace[3].

There is nothing strikingly remarkable in the fact that a strange novelty should excite curiosity and wonder. However, one must remember that the Chinese were not given to admiration for foreign people and foreign products. They were actually inclined to dismiss anything which was not Chinese. True, Chinese culture had always been deeply concerned with time and astronomy and the fascination exerted by the Western mechanical clock on the cultivated Chinese, may be supposedly related to this fact. Yet, if I am not mistaken, the Chinese of the sixteenth, seventeenth and eighteenth centuries did not emphasize the connection between the Western clock and the study of the heavens[4]. Essentially they regarded the Western clock as a toy and only as a toy. One perceives in their attitude toward the 'self-ringing bells' the same kind of feelings that the gadgets of Archimedes and Heron aroused among the ancient Greeks and Romans[5].

At the end of the sixteenth century, the Florentine merchant, Carletti, noticed that the Chinese had no interest whatsoever in European products but that they 'bought lenses of all sorts, and especially coloured ones. But above all things they valued those triangular-shaped glasses which show the delights of various colours when one looks through them toward the open air in the country or else-where, and in which one sees the reflections of many things. And these were sold at up to 500 ducats each, and such was the wonder with which they struck those people the first time that they saw them that they began to praise them aloud, saying that what one saw by means of them was the matter from which the heavens are made'[1]. While the Europeans were using lenses to produce microscopes, telescopes, and spectacles, the Chinese delighted in using them as charming toys. They did the same with clocks. Lenses, clocks, and other instruments had been developed in Europe to satisfy specific needs felt by European society in response to problems set by the European socio-cultural environment. In China the contrivances fell unexpectedly out of the blue and quite naturally the Chinese regarded them merely as amusing oddities.

Intellectuals were trained in art and philosophy, not in the sciences. As Father Ricci noticed, 'no one would labour to attain proficiency in mathematics or in medicine who had any hope of becoming prominent in the field of philosophy'[2]. Urban life did not set the tone of the national culture. In a society composed essentially of an upper class of *literati* trained in the humanities and of a large mass of peasants who, as Dr. Chiang puts it, 'counted their time in days and months, not in minutes or hours'[3], the clock had little chance to play the role of a useful, practical con-trivance. For this to happen, a complete change of society, of its structure and of its needs had to occur.

A machine has a practical meaning only as an expression of man's response to the problems set by his environment and by his fellow men. The Chinese could grasp the usefulness of machines pertaining to irrigation, for example, but could not understand the purpose of other Western inventions[1]. Even at the end of the eighteenth century, the compilers of the *Ssu—K'u ch'üan—shu ti—yao* wrote that 'In regard to the learning of the West, the art of surveying the land is most important, followed by the art of making strange machines. Among these strange machines, those pertaining to irrigation are most useful to the common people. All the other machines are simply intricate oddities, designed for the pleasure of the senses. They fulfil no basic needs'[2].

The Chinese economy and society did not substantially change for centuries after the arrival of the Portuguese, and in China the clock remained for centuries a curious toy. In 1769 Father Jean Mathieu de Ventavon wrote: 'I have been appointed by the Emperor as clockmaker, but I should rather say that I am here as a machinist because the Emperor expects me to produce not really clocks but curious machines and automata'[3]. Van Braam, who led a Dutch embassy to Peking at the end of the eighteenth century, wrote that one day the highest in rank among the mandarins showed him 'a common square bottle which he had brought with him and in which there was a little wooden mill, turned by fine sand falling through a kind of funnel at the top of the bottle upon the ladle boards of the wheel. In short, it was one of those playthings which are to be found in a thousand different shapes and to be purchased for a trifle in a European fair. He asked me if I was acquainted with this piece of mechanism. I told him that I had seen a great number, and of a much handsomer external form. He then asked me why we had brought with us nothing of the same kind. I observed in answer that as in our country they only serve for the amusement of children, we had not supposed that they would give the least pleasure or excite the smallest attention. He assured us of the contrary, and spoke in the language of a man who thinks himself the possessor of a wonder'[1]. De Guignes, the secretary of van Braam, reported the same episode and added that 'one should bring to Peking especially those playthings that European boys use to amuse themselves. Such objects will be received here with much greater interest than scientific instruments or *objets d'art*. . . . When Chinese people buy at great expense some mechanical pieces in Canton, they do it not in order to use them for the purpose for which they were constructed but rather to use them as toys and amuse themselves'[2]. A few years later, C. Abel observed that 'in every part of China through which the (English) Embassy passed, watches were considered as objects of the greatest curiosity. The attendants of the Embassy were perpetually requested to dispose of theirs. I was not, however, able to ascertain whether they valued them as markers of time or simply as curious baubles'[3].

4—According to a long-established belief, in 1550 St. Francis Xavier presented a clock to Yoshitaka Ouchi, governor of Yamaguchi; this is believed to be the first mechanical clock of European making to reach Japan. About forty years later there is a record of the presentation of a clock to Hideyoshi (*d.* 1598) in Kyoto by another missionary. A clock made in Madrid in 1581 was presented to Ieyasu (*d.* 1605) again by a missionary[4].

Both in China and in Japan, the example of the missionaries was soon followed by merchants who gave

precious clocks to influential people in order to obtain
trading licences and commercial privileges. When embassies
were sent from Europe to Asia, clocks of extraordinary
craftsmanship and ingenuity were usually included among
the presents to be offered to the Asian rulers[1]. Especially
in China, where the bureaucratic organization of the
country offered conditions conducive to abuse and where
both mandarins and eunuchs could be bribed on occasion,
clocks were commonly used as gifts[2]. Failure to present an
influential person with a clock or watch could cause no
little trouble to the Europeans. Father Ricci related that in
1596 one of the judges in Schiaochin 'was very angry with
the Fathers because they did not give or lend to him a
mechanical clock and he did not hesitate to use his authority
to avenge himself . . . he summoned two of the mission's
domestics to his court and had them cruelly whipped'[3].
At the end of the eighteenth century, Barrow related that
the Missionaries 'find it necessary to make frequent, and
sometimes expensive, presents to those (eunuchs) in particular about the person of his Imperial Majesty. Should
any of these gentlemen (the Missionaries) happen to carry
about with him a watch, snuff-box or other trinket, which
the eunuch condescends to admire, there is no alternative;
the missionary takes the hint, and begs his acceptance of it,
knowing very well that the only way to preserve his
friendship is to share with him his property. An omission
of this piece of civility has been productive of great injury
to the Europeans. The gentleman who regulates and keeps
in order the several pieces of clock-work in the palace
assured me that the old eunuch, who was entrusted with
the keys of the rooms, used to go in by night and purposely
derange and break the machinery, that he might be put
to the trouble and expense of repairing it. This happened
to him so often that, at length, he became acquainted with

the secret of applying the proper preventive, which although expensive was still less vexatious than the constant reparation of the mischief done to the articles of which he had the superintendence'[1].

Until the beginning of the eighteenth century, clocks were used almost exclusively as gifts and only rarely were they the object of commercial transactions. The Court Minutes of the East India Company in London and the China Factory records give no evidence that clocks and watches were exported by the Company to China during the latter half of the seventeenth century. The English customs books of the same period show exports of time-pieces to Sweden, Denmark, Germany, Holland, Flanders, Italy, Russia, Turkey, New England, the Barbados, and many other places, but none at all to China or Japan[2]. The records of the Dutch East India Company show that throughout the seventeenth century only a few timepieces were sent to Japan and most of these were gifts[3].

The fact of the matter was that not many people in China and Japan could afford the expensive self-ringing bells and those who could afford them, were, especially in China, in the position of getting them as gifts. This state of affairs suddenly changed in the first decades of the eighteenth century when Europe began the production of low-priced timekeepers and the English, soon followed by the Swiss, began to export them to Canton. In the 1730's Father Duhalde wrote that the Europeans 'imported formerly (to Canton) cloths, crystals, swords, clocks, striking-watches, repeating clocks, telescopes, looking-glasses, drinking glasses, etc. But since the English come regularly there every year, all these merchandises are as cheap there as in Europe'[4]. There is exaggeration in Father Duhalde's statement[5] but it cannot be denied that after the beginning of the eighteenth century the export of European clocks and watches particularly to China, enjoyed a sudden and remarkable expansion[1]. By 1775 it was remarked that 'the Chinese receive now watches through Canton at good prices' and about 1805 a French observer noticed that 'watches are now sold in China at a very low price. . . . I have seen watches for more than 100,000 *livres* being sent back to London and an equal amount is still here unsold. The Swedes and the Danes have imported so many watches that these are now sold in the Chinese shops at 5 piastres the pair. Almost all these timepieces come from Switzerland'[2].

Museums and private collections contain a large number of priceless and elaborate timekeepers that were produced in Europe for the Chinese market[3]. These pieces, however, are a biased sample of what was actually exported to China. Extremely ornate clocks, pornographic watches, *et similia* were brought into the Heavenly Kingdom and at the end of the eighteenth century a sumptuary law tried to put an end to this trade[4]. But sources agree that the expansion of the European export trade in the eighteenth century was largely due to the sale of cheap pieces. A Swedish traveller related in the early 1750's that 'the Chinese buy large and little watches of the English. In their shops they have sometimes English watches to sell, and sometimes at moderate prices, but mostly of the worst kind'[5]. The situation lasted until the end of the eighteenth century when Barrow noticed that 'the gaudy watches of indifferent workmanship fabricated purposely for the China market and once in universal demand, are now scarcely asked for. One gentleman in the Hon. East India Company's employ took into his head that cuckoo clocks might prove a saleable article in China, and accordingly laid in a large assortment, which more than answered his most sanguine expectations. But as these wooden machines were constructed for sale only and not for use, the cuckoo clocks became all mute long before the second arrival of this gentleman with another cargo. His clocks were now not only unsaleable, but the former purchasers threatened to return theirs upon his hands, which would certainly have been done, had not a thought entered his head, that not only pacified his former customers but procured him also other purchasers for his second cargo: he convinced them by undeniable authorities that the cuckoo was a very odd kind of a bird which sung only at certain seasons of the year, and assured them that whenever the proper time arrived, all the cuckoos they had purchased would once again tune their melodious throats'[1].

5—Far more timepieces were brought to China than to Japan, both as gifts and as objects of trade. This was due not only to the fact that the population of China was noticeably greater than that of Japan, but also to the fact that the Japanese had learned to make mechanical clocks on their own.

When Western clocks and Western firearms appeared in the Far East, the fanciful Chinese were fascinated by the clocks while the warlike Japanese were especially fascinated by the guns. The Japanese soon began the manufacture of arquebuses and apparently produced them in fair quantity[2]. Only much later did they become interested in clocks, and then a ticklish problem presented itself. The European clock was based upon a system of twice twelve hours of equal length, whereas the Japanese reckoned time according to the 'natural' day in hours of variable length. Time from sunrise to sunset was divided into six hours, and so was the time from sunset to sunrise. The result of course was that during the summer, daytime hours were 'long' and night-time hours were 'short', while during the winter the opposite was true. Only in the second half of December were the hours of day and night of equal length[1]. Western clocks were obviously unsuited to this system of reckoning time[2].

One can easily recognize three phases in the early history of the production of Japanese clocks. In the beginning, Japanese mechanics produced only a few slavish copies of European clocks without even trying to adapt the mechanism of the clocks to the native system of time measurement[3]. It is commonly asserted by Japanese antiquarians that the first clock made in Japan was produced toward the end of the sixteenth century by Tsudo Sukezaiema, a smith who made a faithful replica of the Western clocks that had been presented to Ieyasu[4]. Early in the seventeenth century, the Japanese craftsmen replaced the European hour circle and its Roman numerals by one giving the twelve Chinese signs of the zodiac and their corresponding numerals, but essentially the clocks they produced were still slavish replicas of European clockwork. A second phase opened up sometime in the course of the seventeenth century when some of the old clocks were 'converted' to a new style of motion work. The fixed hour circle with its revolving centre was removed and a revolving circle was substituted with adjustable 'hour' plates and a fixed hand. Finally, toward the end of the century, the Japanese mechanics devised the double escapement clock with one balance for the hours of the day and a second balance for the hours of the night[5]. By then the Japanese had developed a style of their own and produced clocks that were peculiarly suited to their system of reckoning time, even though they always used the Western principle of the verge and foliot device. Three types of weight-driven lantern clocks were made. The first one, hung by a silk cord or hook, was the wall-clock; the second, mounted on a truncated cone, down which the weights could hang unseen, was the pyramid type; the third placed on a table was known as the table clock (see illustration facing p. 81). Besides these types, the Japanese originated a type of clock called 'pillar clock', because it was designed to be hung from the wooden pillars which supported the roofs on Japanese houses. Japan's paper walls were too fragile to support heavy Western-style wall clocks. The pillar clocks unlike any other clock told the time vertically. A hand fixed to the weight as it descended showed the time on a rod marked with adjustable hours (see illustration facing p. 81). Later on, the Japanese craftsmen developed also very beautiful, pocket-sized Inro watches. These watches were made of brass, key-wound, and fitted into a traditional Japanese Inro, or pillbox case, which was attached to an adjustable cord. Since Japanese dress does not have pockets, Inros were worn around the neck or tucked into the *obi sash*[1].

Most of the Japanese clocks were made in Nagasaki, the gateway through which Western products and ideas continued to creep into the country even after Japan was closed to foreigners in the 1620's and 1630's. Clocks were occasionally produced also in Kyoto the 'city of nobles, artisans and craftsmen,' Edo (Tokyo) the 'city of *samurai*', Osaka the 'city of merchants', and the castle towns of Sendai and Nagoya[2]. Needless to say, Japanese clock manufacturing never came close to the European development of the industry, neither for quality nor for quantity. The production of timepieces was always very small because the feudal structure of society and the unbalanced distribution of income set narrow limits to the demand for clocks. Almost all the '*Wadokei*' (the Japanese clocks) were specifically made for the local *daimyōs* and *shōguns*[3]:

numerous clocks could be found in the castles[1] but there were almost none elsewhere[2]. The number of artisans capable of producing clocks was always very small and those who made them were usually skilled smiths who on occasion turned out timepieces[3]. Even with all these severe limitations, the situation in Japan differed from that prevailing in China. In China, as we have seen, a factory for the production and repair of timepieces was established in the Imperial Palace at Peking at the end of the seventeenth century, but this enterprise retained a typically bureaucratic nature and it remained for a long time an isolated, centralized undertaking[4]. In the 1750's P. Osbeck remarked that 'watchmakers are very much wanted here (in China)'[5]. In 1769 Father Jean Mathieu de Ventavon (1733-1787) reported that 'the Princes and the dignitaries of the Empire call upon the Europeans to have their numerous clocks and watches repaired. . . . We are indeed overloaded with work'[6]. In 1775 it was noticed that the Chinese 'sell damaged watches to the Russians at very low prices because they have no craftsmen capable of repairing them'[7]. At the end of the century it was to his 'great astonishment' that van Braam saw that in one town there were 'three watch-makers' shops'[8]. By then the craft of horology was taking firm root in Canton and around 1800, indulging in exaggeration, J. Barrow wrote that the Chinese 'now fabricate in Canton as well as in London and at one third of the expense all those ingenious pieces of mechanism which at one time were sent to China in such vast quantities from the repositories of Coxe and Merlin'[9]. However, in contrasting the history of Chinese and Japanese horology, one can hardly fail to notice that in China the art of clock-making developed at a much later date than in Japan; in China it failed to produce anything original, and it remained essentially limited to the area of Canton.

The reasons for the different response of the Japanese and the Chinese to Western technology are not easily analyzed. In the case of firearms, it is obvious that the Chinese were not interested in weapons and military matters while the Japanese were[1]. In the case of clocks, the situation was completely different. The Chinese were very interested in clocks, much more so than the Japanese. It may be argued that the Japanese took a less picturesque and more utilitarian view of the clock than did the Chinese, but the available evidence does not support this view[2].

It has been said repeatedly that the Chinese traditionally regarded their country as the centre of the world while the Japanese were not hampered by self-centred cultural pride[3]. The Chinese however, were fascinated by the 'self-ringing bell' and one may submit that, since they were unaccustomed to absorb foreign ideas, they could simply produce unimaginative replicas of Western specimens[4]. The Japanese, on the other hand had a long tradition of absorbing foreign ideas and instead of merely copying the Western clock, were actually able to adapt it to their own needs and to create pieces of unmistakable originality[5].

Other reasons may be tentatively adduced to solve this cultural puzzle. I have already indicated that the Japanese used to measure time in hours of variable length. This system of 'unequal hours' had once been in use in Europe[6] and China as well[7] but in both places it had been abandoned long before the sixteenth century[8]. European clocks could easily be made to measure the time in China (although the Chinese divided the day into 12 rather than 24 equal hours)[9] but they were not suitable to the Japanese system of reckoning time. Thus, resorting to Toynbeean terminology, one could say that the Japanese were confronted with a challenge that the Chinese ignored. The different social structures of the two countries may also be taken into consideration. In both China and Japan craftsmen were not lacking. In regard to China, Brusoni in the seventeenth century wrote that 'the Chinese craftsmen are very skilled in manual work and especially in working ivory, ebony and amber. . . . In mathematical things they are inferior to the Europeans. However, they are capable of making mechanical table clocks and they would make also small ones if they were paid as our craftsmen are'[1]. As far as I know, Brusoni never went to China and he was passing on second-hand information[2], but his statement was not unrealistic. There are no reasons to believe that human skills in China were in greater scarcity than in Japan, but there are reasons to believe that the mandarinate and the bureaucratic structure of the state hindered the unfolding of the potential capacities of Chinese craftsmen. Father Ricci noticed that 'not always the Chinese craftsmen strive to reach a perfection of workmanship. . . . This seems to be particularly noticeable when they toil for the magistrates who compel the craftsmen to work for them at a pay inferior to the usual'[3]. By the use of authority one may force craftsmen to work and to produce things according to traditional patterns, but it is much more difficult to force a man to be inventive and original. Effective demand expressed in monetary terms can be substituted in human affairs with other rewarding stimuli. But in old China this was not the case. The attitude of the mandarins toward the Chinese craftsmen can not be simply disregarded as one of the innumerable examples of abuse of power on the part of bureaucrats. There was more to it than that. The set of socio-cultural values prevailing in Ming China actually penalized craftsmen and craftsmanship. As has been rightly said, 'the difference between artists and artisans was almost a difference of race' and 'a learned Chinese examining the work of an

99

artisan will speak of it with the same astonishment as he would if he examined, say, the intelligent work of a beaver'[1]. The set of social values prevailing in Ming Ch'ing China favoured the oppression of craftsmen and obstructed the progress of applied sciene and technology[2]. The relationship between the Japanese feudal lord and the craftsmen in the village below his castle was seemingly much more productive than the exacting bureaucratic relationship between the temporarily appointed mandarin and the craftsmen of the Chinese village[3].

To me, however, a most important factor was the size of the two countries and the isolation in which most of the Chinese population lived. Macao was a Portuguese trading post and in Canton the natives were largely exposed to Western influences[4]. But the rest of the country lived in virtual isolation. As Nieuhoff saw it, 'why these people who are ingenious and witty enough in some things are so dull and inexperienced in others, proceeds in all probability from their general averseness to deal with foreigners; it being a rule among them, to prohibit them entrance into their country, at leastwise not to admit them farther than their utmost frontiers[5]. With the consolidation of Tokugawa rule, Japan adopted a strong policy of national isolation. In 1623 the English voluntarily left Hirado. In 1624 all Spaniards were driven from Japan and all intercourse with the Philippines was stopped. In 1636 Japanese were forbidden to go abroad and those abroad were not allowed to return. In 1638 the Portuguese were expelled and when they sent an embassy in 1640 to re-open trade, almost the whole party was summarily executed. However, the Dutch traders were allowed to keep a trading station on the islet of Deshima in Nagasaki Harbour. Through this umbilical cord European influences continued to creep into Japan as they were creeping into China through Canton. In China, however, there were about 150 million people[1] and internal communications with Canton were generally poor. In Japan there were less than 25 million people[2] and the network of roads and internal communications was relatively good. Despite the more intransigent and hostile policy of the Japanese government, foreign ideas and techniques could make an inroad into Japan from Nagasaki much more easily than they could into China from Canton[3].

All the preceding remarks are by necessity fragmentary and it is difficult to say whether or in what measure each fragment is relevant to the question of the differing responses of China and Japan to the impact of Western technology. On a more general level one may recall that Tokugawa Japan had flourishing urban centres such as Edo, Osaka and Nagasaki where a vigorous merchant class asserted and expressed itself in an ebullient urban culture that reached its apogee in the Genroku Years (1688-1704)[4]. Nothing similar occurred in China where the tone of the culture in towns was always agricultural and bureaucratic[5]. Such considerations, however, do not answer the original question; they widen it. The fact of the matter is that the answer to the question is bound to be vague and imprecise because the question itself is vague and its legitimacy on the historical plane is rather questionable. When we ask 'why did China not *succeed* in producing clocks and guns' and 'why did China not *succeed* in moving toward industrialization' we implicitly assess Chinese performance on non-Chinese terms. But, as Collingwood wrote, we cannot justifiably assume 'that two different ways of life were attempts to do one and the same thing ... Bach was not trying to write like Beethoven and failing; Athens was not a relatively unsuccessful attempt to produce Rome'. We should perhaps paraphrase a statement by one of the directors of the Rockefeller Foundation and conclude that 'it is not only rather graceless, but rather pointless to ask why in the course of the sixteenth, seventeenth and eighteenth centuries China did not develop European technologies. The wonder is that such things occurred at all.'

EPILOGUE

It has been argued that the invention of the mechanical clock came in response to the European climate because during the winters the water in the clepsydras froze and the clouds all too often rendered the sundials useless. Such an explanation exemplifies the kind of simplistic determinism which unfortunately one encounters so often in history books. As has been repeatedly indicated in the previous pages, the first mechanical clocks kept time so imperfectly that they had to be continually adjusted, the corrections being made by governors who turned the hour hand backward or forward precisely on the basis of sundials and water clocks. Thus the first mechanical clocks cannot absolutely be regarded as substitutes for sundials and water clocks.

The reason "why" Europeans produced the mechanical clock is much more subtle. As P. G. Walker wrote some years ago:

"Because we see the machine reshaping society and changing man's habits and ways of life, we are apt to conclude that the machine is, so to speak, an autonomous force that determines the social superstructure. In fact, things happened the other way around . . .The reason why the machine originated in Europe is to be found in human terms. Before men could evolve and apply the machine as a social phenomenon they had to become mechanics".

The men of the thirteenth century thought of measuring time in mechanical terms because they had developed a mechanical outlook of which the mills and the bell-ringing mechanisms were abundant and significant evidence.

Soon after its appearance, the clock assumed the role of a status symbol. In Europe, towns competed with one another in the construction of the most lavish clocks and many of these municipal timepieces possessed elaborate movements and dials whose meaning very few could understand. Soon after the portable clock appeared, it became fashionable for kings and nobles to have the faces of these contrivances painted in their portraits. At the same time, the machine which had been devised to satisfy particular human needs created new ones. Men began timing activities that, in the absence of clocks, they had never thought of timing. People became very conscious of time, and, in the long run, punctuality became at the very same time a need, a virtue, and an obsession. Thus a vicious circle was set into motion. As more and more people obtained clocks and watches, it became necessary for other people to possess similar contrivances, and the machine created the conditions for its own proliferation.

At the same time, clocks and watches were insistently changing man's way of life and of thinking. Slowly but irresistibly hours of equal length were substituted in Europe for the unequal hours and other time divisions which were more closely connected with the seasons. A long time passed before references to 'the time of the first mass' or 'the time of the vespers' were completely abandoned; but the reference to the more abstract hours 'of the clock' (i.e. o'clock) of equal length gained progressively more ground and eventually prevailed[1]. In Japan the mechanical clock was first adapted to the local tradition of the 'unequal' hours but eventually the mechanically more precise

European solution was adopted. The impact which the clock had on philosophy and art was no less important. There are always, of course, rebellious non-conformists who oppose prevailing trends. Just after the first clocks appeared, a Welsh poet, Dafydd, wrote in the second half of the fourteenth century:

Woe to the black-faced clock on the ditch-side which awoke
    me
A curse on its head and tongue, its two ropes and its wheel,
Its weights, heavy balls, its yards and its hammer,
Its ducks which think it day and its unquiet mills.
Uncivil clock like the foolish tapping of a tipsy cobbler,
A blasphemy on its face . . . a dark mill grinding the night[2].

Centuries later, Madame Louvigny left her residence in Rue Ville-du-Temple in Paris, because the clocks of the 'Hostel d'Epernon' had been set with a mechanism that struck the hour, the half hour, and the quarter. In her opinion, all those strokes 'cut her life into too many little pieces'[3]. But such attitudes were notable exceptions. In Europe where the clock soon became an essential object of everyday life, the modes of thinking of the people as well as their ways of expression, were deeply influenced by it. Froissart, who thought that

    L'orloge est, au vrai considerer
    Un instrument très bel et très notable

wrote a poem of 1174 verses in which he developed an analogy between the mechanical movements of a clock and the sensations and movements of a loving heart[1]. One century later, another poet, Gaspare Visconti, wrote a shorter and more delicate poem in which again feelings of love are compared to the movements of a clock[2]. These might be judged extravaganzas of mechanically inclined poets, but in the course of the sixteenth and seventeenth centuries the clock as a machine exerted deep influence on the speculations of philosophers and scientists. Kepler asserted that 'The universe is not similar to a divine living being, but is similar to a clock'. Robert Boyle wrote that the universe is 'a great piece of clock work', and Sir Kenelm Digby wrote again that the universe was nothing but an immense clock. In the framework of this prevailing mechanistic *Weltanschauung*, God was described as an outstanding clockmaker[3].

Per se, these facts may seem to be of interest only to the erudite collector of historical oddities. Their meaning, however, acquires a new dimension when one notices that similar facts are quite common in the history of technology and machines. Each new machine that appears creates new needs, besides satisfying existing ones, and breeds newer machines. The new contrivances modify and shape our lives and our thoughts; they affect the arts and philosophy, and they intrude even into our spare time influencing our way of using it[4].

The machine is a tool. But it is not a 'neutral' tool. We are deeply influenced by the machine while using it. De Saint Exupéry optimistically believes that 'little by little the machine will become part of humanity' and that 'every machine will gradually take on (man's) patina and lose its identity in its function'[5]. However, in a world of machines we too are gradually taking on a patina and are little by little infected by a mechanistic outlook that is not always useful nor beneficial in handling human affairs. As Oscar Wilde reportedly said, 'the evil that machinery is doing is that it makes men themselves machines also'.

Only a fool would undiscriminately condemn the machine as such. We desperately need more and better machines, because we desperately need economic and technological development. But we desperately need also a development of our philosophy and of our capacity for handling human affairs so that we can put our machines to good and reputable uses.

APPENDIX

NOTES

BIBLIOGRAPHY

INDEX

APPENDIX

The earliest form of motive power which appealed to the early craftsmen was the falling weight. Today this is still an ideal method as it gives an even and steady pull. How to control this force was the problem and it was solved with the invention of the verge escapement with foliot. As Alan Lloyd wrote, who invented such a mechanism 'no one knows, and no one probably ever will' but 'whatever his name, he was a perfect genius'.

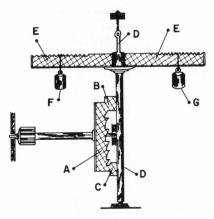

Fig. 1

The verge and foliot device is schematically represented in fig. 1. A wheel with an uneven number of saw-like teeth, known as the crown wheel, A, being driven round by the pull of a weight, one of its teeth comes into contact with the pallet, B, of the 'verge', DD, thus imparting circular motion to the 'foliot', EE, until the tooth escapes past the pallet, B, leaving the crown wheel, A, free to advance. Immediately, however, a tooth on the low side of the wheel, A, finds itself obstructed by the pallet, C, and the process is repeated in the opposite direction. So the 'foliot', EE, swings to and fro, while the teeth of the crown wheel escape past the pallets, B and C, one at a time. The passage of time is measured by the even beats of the balance. The position of the small weights, F and G, determines the resistance that the reciprocating balance exercises upon the crown wheel and its unidirectional movement by the alteration of the position of the weights on the foliot one regulates the speed of the clockwork. As Britten wrote: 'since the design and construction of such an escape wheel from first principles would present considerable problems, it seems not unlikely that the first attempts took the shape of a pin-wheel, the pins projecting at right angles to the surface of the wheel. This arrange-

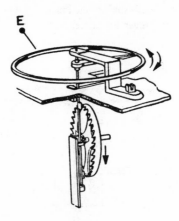

Fig. 2

ment is found in primitive Black Forest clocks quite late into the seventeenth century'.

As one can see in the manuscript by Dondi, very early the 'foliot' was sometimes replaced by a balance wheel. The balance wheel has the same reciprocating action as the foliot (see fig. 2), but with the balance wheel regulation of the speed of the mechanism was effected by alteration of the driving weight. The question of precedence between the balance wheel and the foliot is quite uncertain.

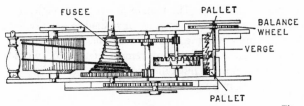

FUSEE   PALLET
BALANCE
WHEEL
VERGE
PALLET

Fig. 3

Fig. 3 shows how the verge escapement was applied to watches. The same figure also shows the *fusée*, i.e. the ingenious device that assured a uniform drive from a spring whose power decreases as it uncoils. The *fusée* is shaped like a truncated cone with spiral grooves which hold a cord in place round it. This cord is joined to the barrel of the main spring. When tightly wound up the spring turns the *fusée* by pulling the cord from the smallest diameter of the *fusée*; when it becomes wound down, it pulls the cord from the larger diameter of the *fusée*. In this way, by pre-adjusting the diameter of the *fusée* to the varying pull of each turn of the spring, the force on the main wheels of the clockwork is uniform.

Fig. 4 shows the form of the verge escapement as later adapted to the pendulum. It consists again of a crown wheel across which is positioned an arbor with two pallets set in it at right

Fig. 4

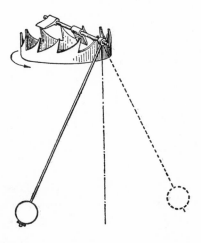

angles to each other. The motive power of a weight or of a spring causes the crown wheel to move unidirectionally, setting the pendulum swinging; on the other hand the swinging of the pendulum controls the movement of the clockwork and measures the time. This is the first and most crude application of the pendulum to clockwork.

NOTES

NOTES TO THE PROLOGUE

PAGE 16

1 Cf. GENICOT, *Evidence of Growth of Population*, pp. 14-29.
2 Cf. LEWIS, *Medieval Frontier*; DUBY, *L'économie rurale*, vol. 1, pp. 139-69; SLICHER VAN BATH, *Agrarian History*, pp. 132-6 and 151-9. One has also to remember that because of insecure conditions the land abandoned in the Dark Ages was not necessarily of a marginal quality. More orderly conditions after the eleventh century permitted the recovery of excellent land.
3 Cf. DUBY, *L'économie rurale*, pp. 170-202; WHITE, *Medieval Technology*, pp. 39-76; DUBY, *Le problème des techniques agricoles*. If the rural sector was able to sustain a rapidly growing urban population and the conditions of the rural population did not deteriorate, we have to admit decisive improvements in the productivity of the agricultural labourers.

PAGE 20

1 See for all WHITE, *Medieval Technology*.
2 FINLEY, *Technical Innovation*, pp. 29-45.

PAGE 21

1 Cf. OLSCHKI, *Guillaume Boucher*, pp. 95ff and bibliography quoted there.

PAGE 22

1 Cf. the general remarks by S. L. Thrupp in *Cambridge Economic History*, vol. 3, pp. 244ff and the abundant biblio-

graphy quoted. In Eastern Europe, however, the feudal aristocracy eventually succeeded in breaking down the power and demands of the guilds and this fact accounts for much of the peculiar social and economic development of Eastern Europe. On this cf. among many, CARSTEN, *Medieval Democracy*.

2 Cf. WHITE, *Medieval Technology*, pp. 79*ff*. At p. 124*n*. 5, White refers to the new types of mechanical mills made in Milan in the middle of the fourteenth century. The chronicler Galvano Flamma emphasized the fact that each one of these mills could be operated by one young man only, '*et non est opus nisi unius pueri*', G. FLAMMA, *Opusculum*, ed. L. A. MURATORI, *Rerum Italicarum Scriptores*, 12, col. 1038. Again in Milan new contrivances for cutting stones were adopted in 1402. It was pointed out that the new mechanism made it possible to use a horse instead of four men and it was calculated that the use of a horse cost three shillings a day while the daily wage of four men amounted to more than fifty-three shillings (*Annali della Fabbrica del Duomo*, vol. 1, p. 248).

PAGE 24

1 RETI, *Francesco di Giorgio Martini*, pp. 287–98.

PAGE 25

1 Keller's *A Theater of Machines* delightfully shows how an extravagant interest in machines and their potential arose in Renaissance Europe.

PAGE 26

1 WRIGHT, *The Works of Liudprand*, pp. 207–8.
2 On the automata in the Byzantine Empire and Liudprand's story cf. BRETT, *Automata*, pp. 447–87, and also OLSCHKI, *Guillaume Boucher*, pp. 89*ff*.
3 OLSCHKI, *Guillaume Boucher*, p. 95. The famous mechanical water clock of the fourteenth century at Fez, Morocco, is,

according to de Solla Price (*Mechanical water clocks*, p. 601),
'completely in spirit with . . . the texts written by al-Jazari'.
Cf. also Chapuis and Droz, *Automata*, pp. 38*ff.* and DE SOLLA
PRICE, *Automata*.

4 On the change of the Byzantine view of the West in the
course of the fourteenth and fifteenth centuries cf. Sevcenko,
Decline of Byzantium, pp. 176*ff* and Geanakoplos, *A Byzantine
looks at the Renaissance*, pp. 157-62.

PAGE 27

1 LAMBROS, *Ipomnina*, p. 26. On the letter by Bessarion, cf.
also KELLER, *Cardinal Bessarion*, pp. 343-8 and Sevcenko,
Decline of Byzantium, p. 177.

PAGE 29

1 The fact was well known also outside Europe. When the
Tartar chieftains succeeded in capturing 'Teutons' on battle-
fields or in their raids against the West, they sent the German
prisoners to work in mines or employed them in manufacturing arms. Cf. OLSCHKI, *Guillaume Boucher*, p. 5.
2 GUICCIARDINI, *Relazione*, p. 131.
3 Cf. CUNNINGHAM, *Alien Immigrants*, pp. 122, 142 and
passim; HAMILTON, *The English Brass and Copper Industries*,
pp. 1-5; CIPOLLA, *Guns and Sails*, pp. 38-9 and 87, *n*. 2.

PAGE 30

1 Especially in the course of the fifteenth century many German craftsmen moved to Italy. Cf. DOREN, *Deutsche
Handwerker*.
2 On the 'decline' of Italy in the course of the seventeenth
century cf. CIPOLLA, *The Decline of Italy*.

PAGE 31

1 On the economic decline of the southern Low Countries
after the mid sixteenth century cf. PIRENNE, *Histoire de la*

Belgique, vol. 4, pp. 407-33. On the emigration of skilled workers from the southern Low Countries, cf. among others, CIPOLLA, *Guns and Sails*, p. 34, *n. 5*.

2 BABINGER, *Maometto*, pp. 469-505.

3 MORYSON, *Itinerary*, p. 419.

PAGE 33

1 HALL, *The Scholar and the Craftsman*, p. 21.

2 The tendency to discuss the problem in terms of a naïve dichotomy in which full-grown scientists face craftsmen as if they did not belong to the same society and culture is unfortunately enough rather common. Besides the article by HALL, cf. also the contributions by Zilsel and Keller in WIENER and NOLAND, *Roots of Scientific Thought*, pp. 219-86.

3 HALL, *The Scholar and the Craftsman*, p. 15.

4 In the writings of the sixteenth and seventeenth centuries the printing press, gun-powder and the compass are often quoted as great innovations that changed the course of history. This contradicts the statement by Hall that the achievements of applied technology did not 'arrest the attention of the scholarly scientist'.

5 On this cf. JONES, *Ancients and moderns*, pp. 154ff.

PAGE 34

1 CROMBIE, *Medieval and early modern science*, vol. 2, p. 121, and HALL, *The Scholar and the Craftsman*, p. 15.

2 BEN-DAVID, *Scientific Growth*, pp. 462-5. One must admit, however, that many of the 'innovators' had received their education in the Universities and held university degrees.

3 Cf. JONES, *Ancients and Moderns*, especially pp. 154ff.

4 Quoted by JONES, *Ancients and Moderns*, p. 204.

5 JONES, *Ancients and Moderns*, especially pp. 162ff.

PAGE 35

1 BOYLE, *Works*, vol. 6, pp. 287-8.

2 NEEDHAM, *Science and Civilization in China*, vol. 3, pp. 154-5.

NOTES TO CHAPTER I

PAGE 37

1 In the Berlin Museum is preserved an Egyptian shadow-clock that dates from about 1500 B.C. but similar devices for telling the time must have existed long before that date. In the course of time, many types of sundials appeared: equatorial sundials, horizontal sundials, vertical sundials, declinate sundials, azimuth sundials, portable sundials, etc. In the West, mottoes were often inscribed on sundials. The collections of such mottoes (cf. GATTY, *The book of sun-dials*; HENSLOW, *Sundial Booke*; HOGG, *Book of old Sundials*) offer a concentrate of human wisdom.

2 King Alfred's biographer, Asser, whose accounts are fairly well authenticated, relates that Alfred made use of special candles as time-keepers. (WARD, *Time measurement*, p. 11). In A.D. 758 Pope Paul I sent King Pepin a present of a few books '*necnon et horologium nocturnum*' (*Codex Carolinus*, p. 513). At the times of King Lothar (A.D. 954-986), a deacon in Verona made an '*horologium nocturnum*' such as 'nobody had ever seen before' (MURATORI, *Dissertazioni*, vol. 1, pp. 364-5. Cf. also BELGRANO, *Antichi Orologi*, p. 30). King Louis IX (A.D. 1226-70) used candles of given length to measure the time while he was reading (*Vie de Saint Louis*, p. 79) and a similar device was still used by the French King Charles V (A.D. 1364-80) (DE PISAN, *Sage Roy Charles*, vol. 1, p. 609). On Eastern fire clocks cf. BEDINI, *The Scent of time*.

3 Sand-glasses appeared rather late. They were largely used on board ships, for timing the length of sailors' watches and the speed of the ships.

4 Cf. the description of the *clepsydra* sent by Haroun el Rashid to Charlemagne above p. 25. On the elaborate *clepsydrae* made in the Near East and Northern Africa cf. DE SOLLA PRICE, *Mechanical water clocks*, pp. 599-601; OLSCHKI,

Guillaume Boucher, pp. 89ff; CHAPUIS AND GÉLIS, *Monde des Automates*, vol. 1, chap. 3; CHAPUIS and DROZ, *Automata*, pp. 36-40. and DE SOLLA PRICE, *Automata*.

PAGE 38

1 Cf. DE SOLLA PRICE, *Origin of Clockwork*.
2 Some early 'clocks' had neither a dial nor hands and consisted essentially of mechanisms for striking the hours. Such was the first 'clock' installed in the belfry at Ghent in 1377. The whole mechanism was made of timber. Cf. VAN WERVEKE, *L'Horloge*.
3 According to DE SOLLA PRICE, *Science*, pp. 30ff one should 'disentangle the clock from the history of time measurement and connect it instead with the longer and earlier history of astronomical models such as the astrolabe and equatorium'.

PAGE 39

1 Cf. THORNDIKE, *Invention of the mechanical clock*, pp. 242-3; LLOYD, *Outstanding clocks*, pp. 1-8; NEEDHAM, and ass., *Heavenly Clockwork*, pp. 195-6; ZINNER, *Frühzeit der Räderuhr*, pp. 8-11. Prof. Dr. Zinner feels that '*sehr wahrscheinlich*' the mechanical clock was invented in Germany. (ZINNER, *Wurde die Räderuhr in Deutschland oder in Italien erfunden*, pp. 19-22), but the evidence quoted is not conclusive.
2 The first mention of cannon in Europe occurs in a Florentine document of 1326. From that document we learn that the town council had decided to buy some bronze guns and iron gunshot for the defence of the city. If cannon were already in use and could be bought in the 1320's, one may guess that their 'invention' occurred some time toward the end of the thirteenth century.

PAGE 40

1 NEEDHAM and ass., *Heavenly Clockwork*, p. 197.
2 For some information about the places in Europe where the

first public mechanical clocks appeared and the dates at which they appeared cf. ZINNER, *Ältesten Räderuhren und Modernen Sonnenuhren*, pp. 26*ff.* Cf. also ZINNER, *Astronomische Instrumente*, pp. 14*ff.*

3 BELGRANO, *Antichi Orologi*, p. 31.

4 MICHEL, *L'horloge de la Cathédrale de Beauvais*; REVERCHON, *Histoire de l'Horlogerie*, pp. 32-3.

5 FLAMMA *Opusculum* in MURATORI, *Rerum Italicarum Scriptores*, vol. 12, col. 1011; BELGRANO, *Antichi Orologi*, pp. 32-3.

PAGE 41

1 LECOCQ, *Horloges de Chartres*, pp. 295 and 297-9. REVERCHON, *Histoire de l'Horlogerie*, p. 53.

2 For the clock in Padua cf. VERGERIUS and CORTUSIUS, in MURATORI, *Rerum Italicarum Scriptores*, vol. 16, col. 171, and vol. 12, col. 912. For Genoa, cf. STELLA in MURATORI, *Rerum Italicarum Scriptores*, vol. 17, col. 1092. For Bologna, cf. DE GRIFFONIBUS *Memoriale* in MURATORI, *Rerum Italicarum Scriptores*, vol. 18, col. 172. For Ferrara, cf. CAMPORI, *Orologieri*, p. 244. See also BILFINGER, *Mittelalterlichen Horen*, pp. 170-84, and BELGRANO, *Antichi Orologi*, pp. 33-46.

3 VIDIER, *Horloge du Palais*, pp. 95*ff.*

4 FRANKLIN, *Vie privée*, p. 61. On the technical characteristics of the clock installed in 1370 on one of the towers of the Royal Palace in Paris cf. ROBERTSON, *Evolution of Clockwork*, pp. 49-66, and USHER, *Mechanical Inventions*, pp. 202-6.

5 Cf. for instance the document of 1410 regarding the construction of a public clock at Montpellier, and reproduced by REVERCHON, *Histoire de l'Horlogerie*, pp. 60-4; the iron mechanism of the clock was planned to weigh about 2000 pounds, the bell of the clock also about 2000 pounds. In addition there was a striking figure and some other paraphernalia. For the whole thing, the makers estimated a price of 200 'escuts' plus two 'muids de vin' and two 'molons de ble'. Numerous episodes abundantly prove that it was often difficult for a community to find the necessary funds for the construction of a public clock. Among the many instances

cf. FILLET, *Horloges Publiques*, p. 107; VIAL and CÔTE, *Horlogers Lyonnais*, pp. 2-3; Smith, *Scottish Clockmakers*, pp. 235ff.

6 As Froissart wrote in his poem *Li Orloge amoureuses*, pp. 79-80,

> li orloge ne poet aler de soi
> se il n'a qui le garde et qui en songne
> pour ce il faut à sa propre besongne
> un orlogier qui tart et tempre
> diligamment l'administre, et attempre
> le plons relieve et met à leur devoir

In some cases the craftsman who built the clock was appointed governor of the same; in other words when buying a clock one had to buy its maker too. Henry de Vic, who made the clock of the Royal Palace in Paris in 1370, was probably its first governor (VIDIER, *Horloge du Palais*, pp. 98-9); the locksmith Thomas Le Viez, who built the public clock of Dôle (Jura) in the 1480's, was also appointed governor of it (BRUNE, *Dictionnaire*, p. 165; for Besançon, *ibid.*, p. 89 *ad vocem* Du Chemin Anselet); Gian Carlo Rainieri from Reggio, who built the famous clock in the Piazza San Marco in Venice, obtained for himself and his progeny the position of governor of the same clock (MORPURGO, *Dizionario*, p. 157); in Mantua Bartolomeo Manfredi was appointed governor of the clock that he had built in the 1470's (DAVARI, *Notizie storiche*, p. 221); in Liège, the 'smith' Georges Huysman, who made a new clock at the Cathedral of St. Lambert in 1523-7, was later appointed '*maître de l'horloge*' (PHOLIEN, *L'horlogerie au Pays de Liège*, p. 25); in Lyon Daniel Gom built a clock at the town hall in the 1650's and was appointed its governor (VIAL and CÔTE, *Horlogers Lyonnais*, p. 57); Cristoforo Ganzinotto built a public clock in Genoa in the 1660's and was also appointed governor of it (BELGRANO, *Antichi Orologi*, pp. 50-2). It was not easy to replace a competent 'governor'. After the death of Master Thomas, governor of the clock at the University in Pavia, no competent governor was found so that '*ut quibus horis legant doctores, quibus horis audiant scholares incertum est*' (MARIANI, *Vita universitaria*, p. 105).

As GÉLIS, *Horlogerie ancienne*, p. 48, writes, 'the office of a governor of the clock was not a sinecure. Often the governor had to wind up the clock twice a day and he had therefore to climb twice a day to the top of the clock tower; he had very frequently to grease the machine, because the gears were not so smoothly and precisely constructed; he had finally to reset the hand (or the hands) of the clock almost every time this was being wound, because the clock lost or gained much time in the course of half a day'. Master John de Lendenaria knew pretty well that it was not an easy task to be governor of a clock. In the last days of January, 1436, the poor fellow fell from the top of the staircase in the clock tower in Castronovo near Ferrara. Weeks later he was still in bed, with many of his bones broken, his body aching all over: *'adhuc resupinus cum doloribus maximis jacet in lecto'* (CAMPORI, *Orologieri*, p. 262).

7 Well-to-do citizens often left bequests for the making of public clocks or for keeping the existing ones in good order: cf. SYMONDS, *English Clocks*, p. 15.

PAGE 42

1 FROISSART, *Orloge amoureuses*, p. 53.
2 DAVARI, *Notizie storiche*, p. 220.
3 VIAL and CÔTE, *Horlogers Lyonnais*, p. 4.
4 REVERCHON, *Histoire de l'horlogerie*, p. 62.
5 VIAL and CÔTE, *Horlogers Lyonnais*, p. 2, *n.* 5.
6 FILLET, *Horloges Publiques*, pp. 104-5.

PAGE 43

1 This was the case of the clock of the Cathedral at Wells in England. Cf. BRITTEN, *Old Clocks*, p. 12.
2 LLOYD, *Outstanding clocks*, p. 26.
3 VEILLIARD, *Horloges et Horlogers Catalans*, p. 163.
4 SANDOZ, *Les maîtres horlogeurs à Besançon*, p. 32.

PAGE 44

1 UNGERER, *L'Horloge de Strasbourg*, pp. 8-9.

2 RUBBIANI, *L'orologio del Comune di Bologna*, pp. 349-66. The fact was truly exceptional, especially if one considers that even in the two centuries after the Copernican discoveries it was still customary to use the 'Ptolemaic' for astronomical dials as it was easier to use it to indicate the hour as well as other things. As a 'reference', which is the first requisite of a dial, the 'Copernican' system is useless.

3 Cf. UNGERER, *Horloges astronomiques*, and CHAPUIS and DROZ, *Automata*, pp. 49-58.

PAGE 45

1 BELGRANO, *Antichi Orologi*, p. 40.

2 The reference is to Giangaleazzo Visconti, Duke of Milan, Prince of Pavia and Count of Virtú. Giovanni de' Dondi was invited by Duke Galeazzo II to teach at the University of Pavia in 1372 and was again invited to Pavia in 1383 by Duke Giangaleazzo Visconti. As '*medicine doctor*' he also cured Azzo, son of Giangaleazzo. On the life of Giovanni Dondi cf. A. BARZON, *Giovanni Dondi dell'Orologio* in DONDI, *Tractatus Astrarii*, pp. 3-15.

PAGE 46

1 From *Le Songe du Vieil Pélerin adressant au Blanc Faucon à bec et pieds dorés*, by Philippe de Maizières, counsellor to the King Charles V of France. The passage was reproduced in *Histoire de l'Academie Royale des Inscriptions*, 16 (1751), pp. 227-8.

2 Toward the middle of the fifteenth century the Duke of Milan hired an astrologer of good repute, master William of Paris, who 'was in the service of His Highness the King (of France)'. Master William restored in a limited way the 'sphere' of Dondi. Cf. MICHAEL SAVONAROLA in

MURATORI, *Rerum Italicarum Scriptores*, vol. 24, col. 1164, and
the document published by CAFFI, *Castello di Pavia*, p. 550.
On the vicissitudes of Dondi's masterpiece cf. FALCONET,
Dissertation, pp. 400-1, and now MORPURGO, *L'Umanesimo
Padovano e l'Astrario* in DONDI, *Tractatus Astrarii*, pp. 40-1.

3 PETRUCCI, *Il Ms. D. 39 della Biblioteca Capitolare di Padova.
Descrizione e Trascrizione*, in DONDI, *Tractatus Astrarii*, pp.
45-176; FRANCESCATO, *Glossario*, ibid., pp. 177-95; and
the photographic reproduction of the Padua mss. *Ibid.*,
pp. 196ff.; THORNDIKE, *Magic and experimental science*, vol. 3,
pp. 386-97, 740-1; THORNDIKE, *Milan manuscripts*, pp. 308-
17; WHITE, *Medieval Technology*, pp. 125-6.

4 LLOYD, *Outstanding clocks*, p. 24.

PAGE 47

1 WHITE, *Medieval Technology*, p. 126.

2 In order to instal the public clock on the Palazzo del Podestà
in Bologna in 1356 all citizens of twenty years of age and
more were taxed 18 pennies each (DE GRIFFONIBUS, *Memoriale*
in MURATORI, *Rerum Italicarum Scriptores*, vol. 18, col. 172).
In 1386 royal patents authorized the Town Council in Lyon
to levy a tax for the construction of a public clock. On this
occasion, however, a minority of citizens violently opposed
the project (VIAL and CÔTE, *Horlogers Lyonnais*, p. 3). Cases
of taxes for the construction of public clocks in South-
Eastern France are quoted by FILLET, *Horloges Publiques*,
pp. 105-11.

3 LABARTE, *Inventaire*, pp. 278-9, item no. 2598. In the years
1299 and 1300, a Petrus Pipelard alias Perrotus, goldsmith,
was on the payroll of King Philip the Fair 'because he is
constructing a clock for the King' (VIDIER, *Horloge du Palais*,
p. 96). It is not unlikely that the clock made by Pipelard is
the same that later appeared in the collection of Charles V.

4 According to VIELLIARD, *Horloges et Horlogers Catalans*, p.
165, 'the Catalan archives reveal the existence of portable
mechanical clocks already by the middle of the fourteenth
century'. This statement is unfortunately rather vague. In

the payrolls of King Charles V of France one finds, under
the dates 24 November and 23 December 1377, orders of
payment to Pierre de Sainte Béate, *'nostre orlogeur'* respectively for *'un orloge portative'* and *'un petite aurloge'*
(DELISLE, *Mandements*, p. 763, no. 1522 and p. 799 no. 1561).
Pierre de Sainte Béate, we know, was a craftsman who
made mechanical clocks and he, in fact, built most of the
mechanism of the big clock at the Palace of the Popes in
Avignon (MICHEL, *Premières horloges*, pp. 216-17). In the
early 1410's documents relating to the households of
three prominent noblemen in Basel give among various
pieces of furniture, an *'orologium'*, an *'höreley'* and a *'zitglockli'*
(little clock) (FALLET-SCHEURER, *Uhrmackerkunst in Basel*,
p. 73).

PAGE 48

1 DE PISAN, *Charles V*, vol. 1, p. 609.

2 MORPURGO, *Ruote o molle*, pp. 31-2. Cf. also MORPURGO,
   Dizionario, p. 33.

3 MICHEL, *Horloge de Sapience*, pp. 297-8.

4 ZINNER, *Frühzeit der Räderuhr*, p. 17, believes that the clock
   reproduced in a French miniature of 1406 (Bibl. Nat. Paris
   MS. 426) is 'obviously' (*'offenbar'*) a spring driven clock.
   But the miniature does not show the interior of the clock
   nor its mechanism and the statement by Prof. Zinner is
   based only on the external shape of the timepiece. According
   to Prof. Zinner the *'orloge portative'* made in the 1370's by
   Pierre de Sainte Béate (see above note 4 to p. 47) was
   'probably' (*'wahrscheinlich'*) a spring driven clock.

PAGE 49

1 LLOYD, *Outstanding clocks*, pp. 30-2.

2 DOUËT-D'ARCQ, *Comptes de l'hotel des rois*, p. 388.

3 On this portrait cf. GÉLIS, *Horlogerie ancienne*, pp. 4-6.

4 Pocket watches appeared toward the end of the fifteenth or
   at the very beginning of the sixteenth century: on the

question cf. MORPURGO, *L'orologio tascabile*; REVERCHON, *Histoire de l'horlogerie*, pp. 67-8. Cf. also below note 2 to p. 61. Clocks were also collectors' items. In the art collection of Florimond Robertet (1457-1532), minister to King François I, there were 'twelve clocks seven of which strike the hours . . . and a big one covered with golden leather that shows the planets and the signs and the celestial movements' (GRÉSY, *Inventaire*, pp. 27-8). In the sixteenth century the Emperor Charles V's collection of clocks was very famous.

PAGE 50

1 From the middle of the sixteenth century one finds precious clocks in rock crystal cases and precious watches whose cases are finely chiselled or pierced or painted in enamel. One also finds time-keepers constructed with curious shapes and forms such as clocks in the form of a crucifix (BRITTEN, *Old clocks*, p. 32, plate 16) and watches in the shapes of a cross, skull (BRITTEN, *Old clocks*, p. 55, plates 36 and 37), dog, lion, rabbit or pigeon (JAQUET and CHAPUIS, *Montre Suisse*, plates 12, 13 and 14). Astronomical watches were also made cf. JAQUET and CHAPUIS, *Montre Suisse*, plates 15, 16 and 17.

2 Cf. the remarks by DEFOSSEZ, *Les Savants*, pp. 52-71; LLOYD, *Outstanding Clocks*, pp. 61-9

3 Cf. for instance BERTELE, *Precision Timekeeping*, p. 801.

4 HENRARD, *Documents*, p. 169.

5 FILLET, *Horloges Publiques*, p. 104.

PAGE 51

1 BELGRANO, *Antichi Orologi*, p. 54n.

2 MOTTA, *Musici*, p. 529.
3 BABEL, *Histoire corporative de l'horlogerie*, p. 46.
4 PIERIS and FITZLER, *Ceylon*, vol. 1, p. 299.
5 Among clockmakers one also finds occasionally cutlers (VIDIER, *Horloge du Palais*, p. 98, *n.* 5 and VIAL and CÔTE, *Horlogers Lyonnais*, p. 58), makers of instruments for navigation (VIELLIARD, *Horloges et Horlogers Catalans*, p. 166), and makers of crossbows (CAMPORI, *Orologieri*, p. 247). On Pierre Pipelard, who was goldsmith and clockmaker at the end of the thirteenth century, cf. above footnote 3 to p. 47. Even famous clockmakers were referred to sometimes as 'clockmakers', sometimes as 'smiths'. Heinrich Halder from Basel, who probably made the first clock of Basel cathedral, worked at the clock of Strasbourg cathedral (1372) and constructed the first public clock in Lucerne (1385), is in some documents mentioned as '*horologifex*', sometimes as '*schlosser*' (locksmith) and sometimes as '*fabrum*' (smith) (FALLET-SCHEURER, *Uhrmacherkunst in Basel*, pp. 77-80).
6 LIISBERG, *Urmagare og Ure*, p. 137.
7 SMITH, *Scottish Clockmakers*, p. 125.
8 FALLET-SCHEURER, *Uhrmacherkunst in Basel*, pp. 102-3 and 152-3.
9 RACHEL, *Das Berliner Wirtschaftsleben*, p. 197.
10 VIELLIARD, *Horloges et Horlogers Catalans*, p. 166.
11 LLOYD, *Outstanding Clocks*, p. 25.
12 *Calendar of the Patent Rolls*, Edward III, 4 May 1368.

PAGE 52

1 LLOYD, *Outstanding Clocks*, p. 6.
2 MICHEL, *Premières horloges*, p. 215.
3 SIDENBLADH, *Urmakare i Sverige*, p. 9. Petrus Astronomus the monk from Vadstena, who constructed the clock in Uppsala cathedral, was a German by birth and lived in Uppsala in 1506 cf. BRING, *Biography of Polhem*, p. 15.
4 SMITH, *Scottish Clockmakers*, p. 2.
5 Used in this way, the term 'Germany' includes most of Switzerland, the northern and southern Low Countries,

Alsace, Lorraine, Austria and the Tyrol. Cf. also below note 6.

6 On Henry de Vic and his clock at Paris, cf. VIDIER, *Horloge du Palais*, pp. 95-6. Henry de Vic may have been born in Lorraine (then part of the Roman-German Holy Empire) and more precisely in Vic-sur-Seille (Dept. Moselle) or in Württemberg or in the Rhine region (ROBERTSON, *Evolution of clockwork*, p. 50).

On Jehan d'Alemaigne and his work for the Queen of France cf. DE LABORDE, *Notice des émaux*, vol. 2, p. 415. On German locksmiths-clockmakers working in Besançon in the fifteenth and sixteenth centuries, cf. SANDOZ, *Maîtres horlogeurs*, pp. 5 and 7. As late as 1650 German clockmakers were invited to Lyon to help in the construction of an elaborate astronomical clock cf. VIAL and CÔTE, *Horlogers Lyonnais*, p. 56.

7 On German clockmakers working in Lombardy cf. N.N., *Tedeschi in Milano*, p. 997, *n.* 2; P.P., *L'Orologio dell'Ospedale*, pp. 687-8; CANETTA, *Vicende edilizie*, p. 351; etc. On German clockmakers working in Rome and other Italian towns cf. ZINNER, *Wurde die Räderuhr in Deutschland oder in Italien erfunden*, pp. 17-22, and MORPURGO, *Dizionario*, passim. In 1402 in Ferrara a master *Conradus Teotonicus* was in charge of the construction of an elaborate public clock '*cum angelo, tuba, stella et aliis ingeniosis artificiis*'. In the course of time, however, master Conradus realized that he was unable to complete the work and disappeared: '*non capax industriae ad perfectionem concepti magisterii infecto opere se absentavit per fugam*' (DE LAYTO, *Annales*, in MURATORI, *Rerum Italicarum Scriptores*, vol. 18, col. 973).

8 Heinrich Halder from Basel, who probably constructed the clock of the cathedral in his native town (1360's), worked at the clock of Strasbourg cathedral in the early 1370's and constructed the first public clock in Lucerne (1385) (cf. FALLET-SCHEURER, *Uhrmacherkunst in Basel*, pp. 77-80). The first clock of the Royal Palace in Paris was constructed in 1370 by a Henry de Vic from 'Germany' (cf. above note 6). One of the clocks at the papal place in Avignon was

built in 1374-5 by Petrus de Santa Beata, a clockmaker who went to Avignon from Paris for this purpose. The town clock at Angers was built in the 1380's by Pierre Merlin, *'maistre orlogeur'* of the King of France, who sent him to Angers from Paris for this work (MICHEL, *Horloges du Palais Pontifical*, pp. 216-17). In the early fifteenth century master Pierre Cudrifin from Fribourg was invited to Romans (France) to build the public clock (FILLET, *Horloges Publiques*, p. 105). In 1353, however, a public clock was built in Milan and then transported to Genoa. This was actually the first public mechanical clock that Genoa had (cf. BELGRANO, *Antichi Orologi*, pp. 45-6). In the sixteenth century one hears more frequently of large public clocks built in one place and transported to another. The famous clock of the Piazza San Marco in Venice was built in Reggio and then transported to Venice at the end of the fifteenth century (MORPURGO, *Dizionario*, p. 157). For other instances cf. FALLET-SCHEURER, *Uhrmacherkunst in Basel*, pp. 98-9.

9 While in Tuscany in the 1470's, the Marquis of Mantua could not find in Florence a clockmaker capable of repairing his portable clock nor was he able to find a new portable clock on sale in the whole town (BERTOLOTTI, *Arti minori*, p. 290). At the beginning of the sixteenth century there was no craftsman in Geneva capable of repairing the clock of the church of St. Pierre (BABEL, *Histoire corporative*, p. 41), and in Besançon the town's administrators had to call upon a craftsman from Dijon because they could not find in their own town a craftsman capable of repairing the clock of the church of St. Etienne (SANDOZ, *Maîtres horlogeurs à Besançon*, p. 10). In the 1530's the town of Basel had to employ the skilful clockmaker Lienhard Steinmüller in repairing the town clock, although Steinmüller had made fun of the long nose of the Reformator Oekolompad, and was considered a rather litigious and violent man (FALLET-SCHEURER, *Uhrmacherkunst in Basel*, p. 101). If the supply of horological skill was not abundant, neither was the demand for it, and this explains why clockmakers, in general, were hardly men of means. In 1435 the governor of the public clock in

Ferrara was 'very poor' ('*vir pauperrimus*') (CAMPORI, *Orologieri*, p. 246). A clockmaker living in Geneva about 1450 was not in a much better condition (BABEL, *Histoire de Geneve*, vol. 2, p. 109). Of course, craftsmen who worked for Kings or generous Princes may sometimes have enjoyed better economic conditions. For the sixteenth and seventeenth centuries cf. below note 1 to p. 55.

PAGE 53

1   In July 1544 a royal charter was obtained by seven 'master-clockmakers residing in Paris' for incorporating a guild of the clockmakers of Paris (LESPINASSE, *Métiers et corporations*, vol. 3, p. 546 and 549-52). In accordance with the royal charter, a list was prepared with the names of the master clockmakers 'who exercise their profession and have their shops in the town of Paris'. The list indicates also the 'masterpieces' that the masters had produced or had to produce in order to be admitted to the guild. The document (*Archives Nationales* Paris, Y 6⁵, fol. 109), dated September 1545, mentions twenty masters. The names of two are written over with the note 'dead without having produced the masterpiece'. Two other names were, however, added later on to the list. In 1549 there were ten clockmakers in the procession that celebrated the coming to Paris of King Henry II (LESPINASSE, *Métiers et Corporations*, vol. 3, p. 547) but in all likelihood they were not the whole guild. In the 1590's an Italian visitor recorded that there were twenty-two clockmakers' shops in Paris, cf. RAYNAUD, *Paris*, p. 166.

2   The new regulations of the guild ratified in 1646 established that the number of master clockmakers in Paris should be limited to seventy-two (cf. LESPINASSE, *Métiers et Corporations*, vol. 3, p. 555).

3   DEVELLE, *Horlogers Blésois*, pp. 20-1.

4   VIAL and CÔTE, *Horlogers Lyonnais*, pp. 11 and 22.

5   BABEL, *Histoire corporative de l'horlogerie*, pp. 390ff.

6 Cf. p. 65.

7 According to a census of the population of Augsburg in 1610, there were forty clockmakers in the town. Another census of 1615 gives the names of forty-three clockmakers and indication of forty-three journeymen (not citizens). Another census of 1619 gives again the number of forty-three clockmakers. I owe this information to the kindness of Dr. H. F. Deininger, Director of the Staatarchiv in Augsburg.

8 Cf. below notes 5 to p. 67 and 5 to p. 68.

9 For Paris, cf. FRANKLIN, *Vie privée*, pp. 81*ff*; LESPINASSE *Métiers et Corporations*, vol. 3, pp. 546*ff*; for Blois, DEVELLE, *Horlogers Blésois*, p. 38; for Geneva, BABEL, *Histoire corporative de l'horlogerie*, pp. 56*ff*; for Toulouse, DU BOURG, *Corporations de Toulouse* (no. 14), p. 80; for London, ATKINS and OVERALL, *Company of Clockmakers*, pp. 4*ff*; for Lyon, VIAL and CÔTE, *Horlogers Lyonnais*, pp. 22*ff*; for The Hague, HOOGEWERFF, *St. Lucasgilden*, p. 120, and OTTEMA, *Uurwerkmakerskunst in Friesland*, p. 77; for Stockholm, SIDENBLADH, *Urmakare i Sverige*, pp. 10*ff*; for Copenhagen, LIISBERG, *Urmagare og Ure i Danmark*, pp. 183-4.

10 In Basel (Switzerland) the clockmakers were always part of the '*Schmiedenzunft*': cf. FALLET-SCHEURER, *Uhrmacherkunst in Basel*, pp. 95-6, 133-6. Even in Augsburg, where the clockmakers were relatively numerous at the beginning of the seventeenth century (see above note 7 to p. 53), they always belonged to the guild of the Smiths which included twenty-one different kinds of professions (information kindly given to me by Dr. H. F. Deininger). In Nuremberg, according to the general rules prevailing in the town, the clockmakers were never allowed to have a guild of their own. In Edinburgh and Glasgow, where they had been excluded from all guilds, the clockmakers were finally permitted to become members of the Hammermen's Incorporation in 1650: cf. SMITH, *Scottish Clockmakers*, p. xii.

11 In Aberdeen (Scotland) in 1618 there was 'want of skilful men to attend' the public clocks (SMITH, *Scottish Clockmakers*, p. 4). For want of skilful men, in Besançon, Avignon

and Broc et Mayer as late as the 1670's, 1680's, and 1690's, locksmiths and even notaries and school teachers were appointed 'governors' of the local public clocks (GALLIOT, *Horloger en Franche-Comté*, vol. 1, pp. 34ff and 151ff; FILLET, *Horloges Publiques*, p. 116; cf. also SANDOZ, *Maîtres horlogeurs à Besançon*, p. 10). In 1735 it was noticed in Montbéliard that 'in the whole country it is impossible to find a craftsman who could either construct or repair big clocks': a Jean Reichart from Württemberg was consequently invited to Montbéliard to build 'a new clock at the Church of St. Martin' (GALLIOT, *Horloger en Franche-Comté*, vol. 1, p. 147). In Berlin, as late as the 1730's, those who repaired clocks and watches were generally locksmiths: cf. RACHEL, *Berliner Wirtshaftsleben*, p. 197.

PAGE 54

1 During the sixteenth and seventeenth centuries Venice and Rome were perhaps the two places in Italy where professional clockmakers were more numerous. Yet in 1661 and in 1712 there were in Venice only half a dozen '*rolloggieri*' (I owe the information to Prof. D. Beltrami whose *Storia della popolazione di Venezia*, p. 207, *n.* 27, can be consulted; for the year 1712 cf. also FANFANI, *Storia del lavoro*, p. 115). A Venetian report of 1797 (Archivio di Stato di Venezia, *Inquisitorato alle Arti*, B.2) states that in Venice 'clockmakers never had a guild of their own . . . they are less than mediocre and those who actually know how to make a clock or a watch are very rare. Perhaps the fact that there has never been a guild of clockmakers is the cause of the low state of the craft. . . . They mostly repair timepieces rather than make them'. According to the same report, there were in 1797 in Venice twenty-two shops, twenty-nine masters, ten labourers and six helpers. A list of shops existing in Rome in 1622 does not mention any shop of clock or watchmakers (FANFANI, *Storia del Lavoro*, p. 110). The list of taxable people, made in Milan in 1527, does not mention any clock or watchmaker (BARBIERI, *I*

redditi dei Milanesi, pp. 768-9). The census of Florence of 1552 mentions only one '*acconcia oriuoli*': a watch repairer (BATTARA, *Popolazione di Firenze*, p. 56). No clock or watch-makers appear in the censuses of Verona of 1502 and 1616 (FANFANI, *Storia del lavoro*, p. 111).

In Florence, Rome, Venice and Milan clockmakers never had a guild of their own.

2 CAMPORI, *Orologieri*, especially pp. 251-9; MORPURGO, *Orologiai della Volpaia*, pp. 23-6; MORPURGO, *Dizionario*, passim.

3 CIPOLLA, *Economic Decline of Italy*.

4 CAMPORI, *Orologieri*, pp. 249-59; BEDINI, *Johan Philipp Treffler*; BEDINI, *Agent for the Archduke*. The case of Pietro Griffi from Pesaro is typical: he was in the service of the Duke of Urbino in the last decades of the sixteenth century. Griffi was an excellent clockmaker and the Duke forbade him to work for anybody else (MORPURGO, *Dizionario*, p. 99).

5 BRITTEN, *Old Clocks*, pp. 22-64. Britten writes that in the period 1550 to 1650 European clockmakers made no mechanical improvements of any importance, but in this regard one should not overlook the contributions by Jost Bodeker and Jost Bürgi who at the end of the sixteenth century tried to improve upon the traditional escapement cf. ZINNER, *Astronomische Instrumente*, p. 22, and BERTELE, *Precision Time-Keeping*, pp. 794-816.

6 Before the sixteenth century, goldsmiths and jewellers were not so numerous among the clockmakers. In the sixteenth and seventeenth centuries on the contrary, one finds more frequently clockmakers who were also goldsmiths and vice versa (for instance cf. BABEL, *Histoire corporative de l'horlogerie*, p. 43; VIAL and CÔTE, *Horlogers Lyonnais*, p. 12). However, in those centres in which the goldsmiths and the clockmakers had their own separate guilds, the corporative organization generally forbade the combination of both activities, and the guilds quarrelled incessantly (cf. among others BABEL, *Histoire corporative de l'horlogerie*, pp.305-18; VIAL and CÔTE, *Horlogers Lyonnais*, p. 26; DEVELLE, *Horlogers Blésois*, p. 360; GALLIOT, *Horloger en Franche-Comté*, vol. 1, p. 59*ff*; 148*ff* and *passim*).

7 In Venice, toward the end of the sixteenth century, the makers of small clocks and watches did not like to be confused with the makers of big clocks, and according to a report of the Ambassador of Mantua 'they had no wish to soil their hands with big iron clocks' (BERTOLOTTI, *Arti minori della corte di Mantova*, p. 504).

8 Inventories of shops of master-clockmakers of the sixteenth and seventeenth centuries with detailed descriptions of the valuable timepieces kept in the shops have been published for Blois by DEVELLE, *Horlogers Blésois*, pp. 155*ff*; for Geneva by BABEL, *Histoire corporative de l'horlogerie*, p. 512; for Lyon by VIAL and CÔTE, *Horlogers Lyonnais*, pp. 8-9.

PAGE 55

1 Master Gio. Paolo Rainieri who was reputed '*horologiorum artifex optimus*', was greatly favoured by Duke Alfonso I of Ferrara and in 1491, in 1499 and 1505 he obtained for himself and his successors complete exemption from all taxes and duties. Master Cherubino, who, according to Benvenuto Cellini, was '*maestro di oriuoli eccellentissimo*', worked for the Pope in the early part of the sixteenth century. For his good services he was granted a canonry with benefices attached to it (CAMPORI, *Orologieri*, pp. 249-50).

2 Cf. BABEL, *Histoire corporative de l'horlogerie*, pp. 445, 455*ff*. and *passim*. According to Vial and Côte (*Horlogers Lyonnais*, pp. 14 and 21) in seventeenth century Lyon, clockmakers enjoyed satisfactory economic conditions but only a few of them owned the houses where they lived (*ibid.*, p. 19).

3 For Basel, cf. FALLET-SCHEURER, *Uhrmacherkunst in Basel*, p. 154. In seventeenth century Toulouse, clockmakers do not seem to have enjoyed very good economic conditions: cf. DU BOURG, *Corporations de Toulouse* (no. 14), p. 80. In Besançon in 1604 a clockmaker was authorized to keep an inn possibly because his profession as a clockmaker did not give him enough to live on (GALLIOT, *Horloger en Franche-Comté*, vol. 1, p. 39).

4 LESPINASSE, *Métiers et Corporations*, vol. 1, pp. 94-6.

5 OLDEWELT, *De beroepsstructuur van de bevolking der Hollandse*, pp. 81, 82 and 83.

6 Taxes actually paid by watchmakers in Rotterdam and Leiden in 1674 seem to indicate that these craftsmen were generally in the lowest income groups, and not in the second from the top as indicated by the general classification mentioned above in the text. Cf. OLDEWELT, *De beroepsstructuur van de bevolking der Hollandse*, pp. 80ff.

7 Bartolomeo Manfredi, doctor in mathematics and astrology, built the public clock at Mantua, Italy, in the fifteenth century (BERTOLOTTI, *Arti Minori*, p. 289). On Chrètien Herlin and Conrad Dasypodius cf. above p. 57.

8 Also in areas where lay craftsmen were not so rare, friars often dealt with horology. In Forlì (Italy) in 1395 a public clock was built by the Dominican friar Gasparo (BELGRANO, *Antichi Orlogi*, p. 39). In the 1360's in Avignon (France) one of the clocks was made by a friar from Venice (cf. above note 2 to p. 52). On the numerous friars and Jesuits who, in the course of the fourteenth, fifteenth, sixteenth and seventeenth centuries, bothered their heads with horological matters, cf. MORPURGO, *Dizionario*, *passim*.

PAGE 56

1 For Lyon cf. VIAL and CÔTE, *Horlogers Lyonnais*, pp. 29-97; for Blois cf. DEVELLE, *Horlogers Blésois*, pp. 214-450. The high percentage of clockmakers, sons of clockmakers, indicated above in the text is biased and inflated. The reason is that those authors who wrote about the history of horology knew the profession of the father of a clockmaker especially if he too had been a clockmaker. From the biographies compiled by Vial and Côte for Lyon, and Develle for Blois, one also gathers that master-clockmakers very often married daughters of clockmakers.

2 BABEL, *Histoire corporative de l'horlogerie*, pp. 68, 418, 419.

3 BRITTEN, *Old Clocks*, pp. 276, 286, 288.

4 DEVELLE, *Horlogers Blésois*, p. 262.

5 FALLET-SCHEURER, *Uhrmacherkunst in Basel*, pp. 152-3.

6 BABEL, *Histoire corporative de l'horlogerie*, pp. 64-5 and *passim*.

7 BABEL, *Histoire corporative de l'horlogerie*, pp. 80*ff* and 186*ff*; VIAL and CÔTE, *Horlogers Lyonnais*, p. 26.

8 In the guilds the admission fee was lower for the sons of clockmakers than for other applicants (cf. BABEL, *Histoire corporative de l'horlogerie*, pp. 85 and 199). In Paris, the guild's regulation of 1646 established that the number of master clockmakers in the town should not exceed the number of seventy-two and that admission to mastership should be granted 'preferably' to the sons of master clockmakers (LESPINASSE, *Métiers et Corporations*, vol. 3, p. 555, art. 7). Similarly in Blois, the sons of master clockmakers were favoured by the guild regulations and their appointment as master was made easier (DEVELLE, *Horlogers Blésois*, p. 39). For Montbéliard cf. GALLIOT, *Horloger en Franche-Comté*, vol. 1, p. 130).

I have indicated above in the text that most clockmakers who worked in Lyon and Blois in the sixteenth and seventeenth centuries were sons of clockmakers. I should add here that in the sixteenth, seventeenth and eighteenth centuries there were frequent cases of 'dynasties' of clockmakers: one may quote the case of the Montmains, the Nourissons and the Noytolons in Lyon (VIAL and CÔTE, *Horlogers Lyonnais*, pp. 73*ff*, 79*ff* and 85*ff*), the Habrechts from Switzerland (UNGERER, *Les Habrechts*), the Steinmüller in Basel, Switzerland (FALLET-SCHEURER, *Uhrmacherkunst in Basel*, p. 101), the Cupers in Blois, France (DEVELLE, *Horlogers Blésois*, pp. 22-3), the Fromanteels, the Knibbs, the Arnolds and the Perigals in England (BRITTEN, *Old Clocks*, pp. 272-3, 289; PAGE, *County of Middlesex*, vol. 2, p. 160), the Haakmas in Leeuwarden in Friesland (OTTEMA, *Geschiedenis*, pp. 20-2), the Della Volpaia in Florence (MORPURGO, *Orologiai della Volpaia*, pp. 23-6), the Barocci of Urbino (MORPURGO, *Dizionario*, pp. 22-4), the De Befves in Liége (PHOLIEN, *L'horlogerie au Pays de Liége*, pp. 77*ff*).

PAGE 57

1 VASARI, *Vite*, vol. 1, p. 593. Cf. also above note 2 to p. 48.
2 MORPURGO, *Orologiai della Volpaia*, pp. 23-6; MORPURGO, *Dizionario*, pp. 201-4.
3 UNGERER, *Horloge astronomique de Strasbourg*, pp. 14ff.
4 DEFOSSEZ, *Les savants*, pp. 54-5.
5 DEFOSSEZ, *Les savants*, passim.

PAGE 58

1 Some clockmakers collaborated with professional scholars in the construction of planetaria while others prepared special lenses for precision instruments (cf. DAUMAS, *Les instruments scientifiques*, pp. 95-6 and 114). In an Academy founded in Paris in 1726 with the name of *Societé des Arts*, we find, together with professional scientists such as Clairault, Nollet and Rameau, the clockmakers Sully, Julien Le Roy and Pierre Le Roy (VENTURI, *Origini dell'Enciclopedia*, pp. 14-15).

2 In 1586 J. Burgi built a clock that worked with a daily deviation of plus or minus thirty seconds (BERTELE, *Precision Time-Keeping*, p. 801). According to a letter written by Vincenzo Viviani to Prince Leopold de Medici on 21 August 1659, the clockmaker Treffler 'constructed several (clocks) of the greatest accuracy, which demonstrated the time in even more minute divisions, and which in the course of many days did not vary a single minute between them' (BEDINI, *Agent for the Archduke*, p. 155). In a letter dated 24 February 1662 Huygens mentions that one of his clocks 'had functioned for more than four months without varying one minute': this would indicate an average error of half a second every twenty-four hours (DEFOSSEZ, *Les savants*, p. 242). The cases mentioned above indicate degrees of accuracy noticeably superior to those indicated by fig. 1 at the corresponding dates.

Watches were less precise than clocks. As late as 1671

merchants who traded in watches were happy if they could obtain from the master-watchmakers watches that had a deviation of no more than one hour every twenty-four. (JAQUET and CHAPUIS, *Montre suisse*, p. 42). A decisive improvement in the precision of watches came only with the invention of the spiral balance spring in 1675 (BRITTEN, *Old Clocks*, pp. 73-6).

PAGE 60

1 DAUMAS, *Instruments scientifiques*, pp. 155*ff*.
2 Significantly enough, 'the persons' who were 'being by trade Mathematical Instrument Makers . . . were admitted Brethren of the Company of Clockmakers of London' in 1667 (cf. ATKINS and OVERALL, *Company of Clockmakers*, p. 114).
3 CARY, *Discourse on Trade*, p. 21.
4 BABEL, *Histoire corporative de l'horlogerie*, p. 38, *n*. 1.

PAGE 61

1 For Nuremberg, cf. FRISCHHOLZ, *Nürnberg*, pp. 252-3. For Augsburg cf. N.N., *Das Augsburger Uhrmachergewerbe* and ZINNER, *Die Augsburger Uhrmacherei*.
2 A statement made by J. Cochlaeus in 1512 has often been adduced to prove that the pocket watch first appeared at the beginning of the sixteenth century and that its inventor was Peter Henlein of Nuremberg (cf. among others GUMBEL, *Peter Henlein*, and SCHULTHEISS, *Peter Henlein*). Some authors still seem to favour this thesis (cf. ZINNER, *Frühzeit der Räderuhr*, pp. 20-6), but others have convincingly maintained on the basis of solid evidence that pocket watches were made before the times of Peter Henlein (cf. MORPURGO, *Orologio Tascabile*, and REVERCHON, *Histoire de l'horlogerie*, pp. 68-9).

PAGE 62

1   Cf. above note 7 to p. 53.

2   In the 1580's the Danish Royal Family bought many clocks
    made in Nuremberg (LIISBERG, *Urmagare og Ure i Dan-
    mark*, pp. 138-40) and clocks from Augsburg were bought
    by the Swedish Kings (N.N., *Un eccezionale orologio del
    1585*, p. 43).   In the early seventeenth century, Father
    Nicolas Trigault went to Augsburg to get fifteen clocks
    'iustae magnitudinis ut in turribus urbium exponantur' which
    he intended to take to China (LAMALLE, *La propagande du
    P. Nicolas Trigault*, p. 101).

3   GARZONI, *Piazza Universale*, p. 625.   In 1606 the syndics of
    the Church of San Lorenzo in Genoa wanted to have a new
    and better clock for the Church and they decided to look
    for it 'in partibus germanicis' (BELGRANO, *Antichi Orologi*,
    p. 49).

4   MORYSON, *Itinerary*, p. 372.

5   The information was kindly given to me by Dr. Deininger.
    For Nuremberg cf. FRISCHHOLZ, *Nürnberg*, pp. 258-9.   In
    Augsburg there was, however, a good recovery in the second
    part of the seventeenth century and especially in the course
    of the eighteenth century.   Around 1690 and 1720 there
    were in Augsburg between twenty and forty clockmakers
    (N.N., *Augsburger Uhrmachergewerbe*, p. 205) and in the
    first part of the eighteenth century Savary mentions that 'in
    Augsburg there are made many clocks of very common
    quality' (*Dictionnaire*, vol. 3, col. 342).   In a census of 1809
    one finds recorded fifty-six clockmakers.

6   Cf. the numerous telling episodes quoted by DEVELLE,
    Horlogers Blésois.   Cf. also BABEL, *Histoire corporative de
    l'horlogerie*, pp. 46-52, (about Charles Cusin); FALLET-
    SCHEURER, *Uhrmacherkunst in Basel*, p. 101 (about Lienhard
    Steinmüller); MORPURGO, *Origine dell'Orologio Tascabile*,
    pp. 9-10 (about Peter Henlein and his brother), and MOR-
    PURGO, *Dizionario*, pp. 41 and 101 (about Giovanni Giorgio
    Capobianco and a clockmaker of Urbino named Baroccio).
    At the end of the fifteenth century GARZONI, *Piazza*

Universale, p. 625, wrote that: 'The worst habit of these master watchmakers is that just to clean a watch they demand two or three ducats, as if one does not know what they do and what they do not do. With much chatter they tell how they have adjusted the gears, restored the equilibrium, reset the time, put in order many parts of the mechanism, and removed the rust; in short, having timepieces in hand for a month they pretend to have worked on them often, while in fact they just looked at them hanging on a wall or shut in a drawer'. The attitude of Garzoni toward repairs is unchanged today and of course it is not always justified.

7 For Lyon cf. VIAL and CÔTE, *Horlogers Lyonnais*, pp. 20-1. In London, among forty-eight masters who signed a document of the guild in 1632, only three signed with a mark; cf. ATKINS and OVERALL, *Company of Clockmakers*, p. 51.

PAGE 63

1 DEVELLE, *Horlogers Blésois*, pp. 214, 224, 267, 287; BOURRIAU, *Horlogers à la Rochelle*, pp. 15-16.

2 Of course illiterate master-clockmakers were not totally absent: cf. VIAL and CÔTE, *Horlogers Lyonnais*, p. 20, and above note 7 to p. 62.

3 BABEL, *Histoire corporative de l'horlogerie*, p. 419. On the degree of education of clock and watchmakers in eighteenth century Geneva cf. BABEL, *Fabrique genevoise*, pp. 103-4.

4 For Lyon cf. VIAL and CÔTE, *Horlogers Lyonnais*, p. 20; for Paris cf. FRANKLIN, *Vie privée*, p. 144; for Blois, cf. DEVELLE, *Horlogers Blésois*, pp. 426 and 447. La Rochelle was one of the main centres of the Reformation movement in France and significantly enough printing and clockmaking flourished there in the seventeenth century (BOURRIAU, *Horlogers à La Rochelle*, p. 6). Clavelé, a master clockmaker who built a wooden clock, was one of the first Huguenots sentenced to death (FALLET, *Dissertation*, p. 409). For Rouen

in the late seventeenth century, cf. BIANQUIS, *La Révocation de l'Édit de Nantes*, p. xlii.

PAGE 64

1 On the equipment of early clockmakers cf. DEVELLE, *Horlogers Blésois*, pp. 45*ff*; FALLET-SCHEURER, *Uhrmacherkunst in Basel*, pp. 131*ff*; MORPURGO, *Una bottega di orologiai*, pp. 3–5.

2 Other centres of clockmaking developed in the Zaanstreek and in Friesland. Also in these places the French refugees seem to have played an important role in the development of the clock manufactures. Cf. OTTEMA, *Uurwerkmakerskunst in Friesland*, p. 9.

3 BABEL, *Histoire de Geneve*, vol. 2, p. 109.

4 BERGIER, and SOLARI, *Histoire*, pp. 203–9 and 214–24.

PAGE 65

1 Cf. GEISENDORF, *Métiers et conditions sociales du premier Refuge*, pp. 239–49.

2 GEISENDORF, *Métiers et conditions sociales du premier Refuge*, p. 247, *n.* 2.

3 For all that precedes and follows cf. BABEL, *Histoire corporative de l'horlogerie*, pp. 43–88 and 391–3.

4 LETI, *Historia ginevrina*, part 4, pp. 612–13.

5 CUNNINGHAM, *Alien Immigrants*, pp. 140*ff*.

6 CUNNINGHAM, *Alien Immigrants*, p. 138.

PAGE 66

1 MORYSON, *Itinerary*, p. 475.

2 FISHER, *Commercial Trends in Sixteenth Century England*. On Fisher's article see among others STONE, *State control in sixteenth-century England*, p. 108.

3 CUNNINGHAM, *Alien Immigrants*, p. 215. In Scotland, the

Town Council of Aberdeen, on 13th October 1537, dispatched Andrew Cullam to Flanders 'with regard to receiving useful instructions how to keep in order the Kirk clock of St. Nicholas, the Tolbooth and the College orloges'. FLEMING, *Flemish Influence*, vol. 1, p. 339.

4 PAGE, *County of Middlesex*, p. 158; SYMONDS, *English Clocks*, pp. 26-7.

5 BRITTEN, *Old Clocks*, p. 43.

PAGE 67

1 PAGE, *County of Middlesex*, p. 158.

2 BRITTEN, *Old Clocks*, p. 45.

3 BRITTEN, *Old Clocks*, pp. 44-5.

4 SYMONDS, *English Clocks*, p. 30.

5 *Calendar State Papers*, Domestic, James I, 127/15 and 16, January 1622.

PAGE 68

1 ATKINS and OVERALL, *Company of Clockmakers*, p. 2.

2 ULLYETT, *British Clocks*, p. 18.

3 Louis Cuper was still in Blois as late as 1613 when he attended the marriage of his brother Michel (DEVELLE, *Horlogers Blésois*, p. 377). As indicated above in the text, by 1622 he was listed in London among the 'knowne strangers' who made clocks. In 1629 we find him still in London, taking his nephew Abraham Cuper as his apprentice (DEVELLE, *Horlogers Blésois*, p. 378). A 'Josias Cwper Frenchman, denizen clockmaker, was admitted and sworn to the orders of the house (of the Blacksmiths)' in 1628 (ATKINS and OVERALL, *Company of Clockmakers*, p. 3). Other members of the Cuper family moved to England toward the end of the seventeenth century (DEVELLE, *Horlogers Blésois*, p. 432).

4 DEVELLE, *Horlogers Blésois*, pp. 235-6.

5 One of the reasons why the clockmakers of London incorporated in 1631 was that they wanted to control the growing

competition of 'stranger' clockmakers ('for ye restraint of strangers and foreigners' as a document of 1656 explicitly declared: cf. ATKINS and OVERALL, *Company of Clockmakers*, p. 61). In 1630 a number of clockmakers contributed money to pay for the costs of obtaining the charter of incorporation and other expenses (ATKINS and OVERALL, *Company of Clockmakers*, pp. 20-1): the list of contributors contains about fifty names of clockmakers. Among them one finds only three of the 'straingers' clockmakers mentioned in the list of 1622, while one finds eight of the sixteen 'English' clockmakers of the same list. Foreign names are not absent in the list of 1630 and on the other hand one can readily admit that between 1622 and 1630 the number of English clockmakers grew larger in London. Yet, the striking discrepancies between the two lists may possibly indicate that

a) in order to exaggerate the predominance of the 'straingers', not all 'English' clockmakers working in London were mentioned in the list of 1622;

b) only few among the 'straingers' working in London joined the 'English' in the effort to set up a guild of clockmakers. If we admit that the list of 1622 gives a reliable estimate of the number of the foreign clockmakers working in London in that year, and the list of 1630 gives a more accurate estimate of the number of English clockmakers, we may tentatively conclude that in the 1620's there must have been 'within the Citty of London and lyberties thereof or within tenn myles thereof' about sixty or seventy master clockmakers.

By the 1650's, a number of masters complained that the Court of Assistants of the guild was controlled by clockmakers of French origin and 'Frenchmen who are foreigners are admitted to rule the freemen . . . and whereas it was agreed by them lately that if we would bring in a list of those foreigners and strangers by whom we were agrieved they would joine with us in the prosecuting of them, when at a Court we since presented them with a list, they asked us if wee would have them tear out the bowells of ye Companie, soe deare are those strangers and foreigners to them'.

144

(ATKINS and OVERALL, *Company of Clockmakers*, pp. 61-2).

1 BRITTEN, *Old Clocks*, p. 272.

2 FRANKLIN, *La mésure du temps*, p. 140.

3 BRITTEN, *Old Clocks*, p. 280.

4 SAVARY, *Dictionnaire*, vol. 3, col. 334: '*Les Horloges d'Angle-terre sont prohibées en France par deux raisons, la premiére est un ordre du Roi en faveur de la Communauté, et la seconde c'est qu'elles ne s'y vendent pas n'étant pas du goût des François comme celles de Geneve*'.

1 SAVARY, *Dictionnaire*, vol. 3, col. 329-42.

2 BABEL, *Histoire corporative de l'horlogerie*, pp. 91*ff*, notices that the first 'springers' appeared in Geneva after 1660. In Lyon one finds '*faiseurs de ressorts pour les horlogers*' after 1670: cf. VIAL and CÔTE, *Horlogers Lyonnais*, p. 26. In Blois, Antoine de la Garde, clockmaker since 1631, specialized later in the construction of springs; when he died in 1670 he was qualified as '*faiseur de ressorts pour les montres*' (DEVELLE, *Horlogers Blésois*, p. 93).

3 BABEL, *Histoire corporative de l'horlogerie*, pp. 91-109 and 401; DEVELLE, *Horlogers Blésois*, pp. 83*ff*. By the 1680's there were craftsmen in Geneva who specialized in the making of 'instruments for the use of clockmakers' (BABEL, *ibid.*, p. 92).

4 PAGE, *County of Middlesex*, vol. 2, p. 158.

5 GEORGE, *London Life*, p. 173.

6 BABEL, *Histoire corporative de l'horlogerie*, pp. 99 and 101.

7 In seventeenth century Blois, there were two merchants who specialized in the trade of springs for clocks and watches (DEVELLE, *Horlogers Blésois*, p. 93). In the 1690's it was enacted in England that cases and dial-plates should not be exported without the 'works' appertaining to them (ATTON and HOLLAND, *The King's Customs*, p. 143). One of the

reasons for this measure was to prevent anybody except Freemen of London from putting 'London' on their watches and clocks (cf. ATKINS and OVERALL, *Company of Clockmakers*, p. 257). Cf. also JAQUET and CHAPUIS, *Montre Suisse*, p. 43, and for the trade in instruments for clockmakers, *ibid.*, p. 88.

8 BABEL, *Histoire corporative de l'horlogerie*, pp. 495*ff*, and especially pp. 501-2.

1 In the first years of the eighteenth century Christopher Polhem set up at Stjärnsund (Sweden) a clock factory with machines that automatically cut cogwheels and other parts of clockwork. Polhem's factory was set up for mass production. Cf. LUNDWALL, *Stjärnsundsuren*, and SELLERGREN, *Polhem's contributions*, pp. 109-15.

2 SAVARY, *Dictionnaire*, vol. 3, col. 342. Savary also noticed that '*tout le monde n'est pas en état de payer chérément les ouvrages parfaits, et que d'ailleurs la chose est impossible, parce que tous les ouvriers ne sont pas en état d'attendre la perfection*'.

3 SMITH, *Wealth of Nations*, p. 243.

4 SYMONDS, *English Clocks*, p. 59.

5 Cf. above footnote 1.

6 In Great Britain in 1797 a tax was imposed on clocks and watches. The returns to the assessors supply precise information on the diffusion of the use of timepieces among the population of the British Isles. This is the return for the town of Peebles (Scotland): 'In the town of Peebles 15 clocks, 19 silver and 2 gold watches. In the country part of the parish, 4 clocks, 5 silver and no gold watches. In the whole county, town and parish of Peebles included, 106 clocks, 112 silver and 35 gold watches'. (SMITH, *Scottish Clockmakers*, pp. 296-7).

7 SAVARY, *Dictionnaire*, vol. 3, col. 329.

1 For Berlin, cf. RACHEL, *Das Berliner Wirtschaftsleben*, p.

198, and CHAPUIS, *Le Grand Frédéric*. For Russia, cf. *Bolshaia Sovietskaia Entsiklopedeia*, 1950, vol. 47, p. 56. For Stjärnsund in Sweden cf. LUNDWALL, *Stjärnsundsuren*, and SELLERGREN, *Polhem's Contributions*, p. 111. For Ferney cf. BAVOUX, *Voltaire à Ferney*; CAUSSY, *Voltaire, Seigneur de Village*; CHAPUIS, *Voltaire horloger*; and BABEL, *Fabrique genevoise*, pp. 107-25.

2 As has been indicated above (note 1 to p. 53) there were about twenty master clockmakers in Paris in 1545; about the same number was recorded by an Italian who visited Paris about fifty years later. The two sources, however, are of such different nature that any conclusion to be derived from their comparison must be accepted with reservations.

3 LESPINASSE, *Métiers et corporations*, vol. 3, p. 555.

4 Paul Roumieu was an eminent watchmaker from Rouen who emigrated to Edinburgh and reintroduced the art of watchmaking into Scotland. Traditionally Roumieu was supposed to have been one of the refugees driven out of France in consequence of the Edict of Nantes. But it has been now established that he moved to Edinburgh at least eight years before 1685 (SMITH, *Old Clockmakers*, p. 323). In Blois, according to Develle (*Horlogers Blésois*, pp. 9-10), the revocation of the Edict of Nantes caused the departure of some craftsmen but the decline of the craft was already evident in the late 1670's and in the early 1680's.

PAGE 73

1 SCOVILLE, *The Persecution of Huguenots*, passim and especially pp. 434-47.

2 As a matter of fact, French clockmakers who emigrated in search of religious freedom were not a small band. After 1685 one finds them even in Denmark making no small contribution to the development of the Danish clockmaking industry (cf. LIISBERG, *Urmagare og Ure i Danmark*, pp. 169, 174, 176, 178).

3 FRANKLIN, *Mésure du Temps*, p. 144.

PAGE 74

1 SAVARY, *Dictionnaire*, vol. 3, col. 331.

2 JAQUET and CHAPUIS, *Montre Suisse*, p. 29.

3 BABEL, *Histoire corporative de l'horlogerie*, p. 518, *n.* 2 and p. 519. The Swiss were not the only ones to indulge in unfair competition. In 1704 it was reported to the guild of Clockmakers in London that certain persons at Amsterdam were in the habit of putting the names of Tompion, Windmills, Quare, Cabrier, Lamb and other well-known London makers, on their works, and selling them as English: cf. ATKINS and OVERALL, *Company of Clockmakers*, p. 258.

4 GÉLIS, *Horlogerie ancienne*, p. 38.

5 FRANKLIN, *Mésure du Temps*, p. 146.

6 GÉLIS, *Horlogerie ancienne*, p. 38.

PAGE 75

1 GRISELINI, *Dizionario*, vol. XI, p. 4.

2 REVERCHON, *Histoire de l'horlogerie*, p. 151.

3 Cf. below note 5. Later on, in the course of the nineteenth century, Besançon, developed as a great centre of the clock and watch industry, and French output grew in fact larger than the English.

4 On the export of Swiss timepieces all over Europe and overseas in the course of the seventeenth and eighteenth centuries, cf. BABEL, *Histoire corporative de l'horlogerie*, pp. 70 and 516*ff*; BABEL, *L'horlogerie genevoise à Constantinople*, pp. 61-74; SAVARY, *Dictionnaire*, vol. 3, col. 341-2. Cf. also JAQUET ET CHAPUIS, *Montre Suisse*, pp. 121-52 (not very rigorous, however, in the presentation of the historical material). In Constantinople the Swiss clockmakers were already present by the first years of the seventeenth century, and in 1652 it was reported that merchants from Geneva 'live in Constantinople a licentious life and give great scandal'. In 1709 the Swiss colony in Constantinople numbered about fifty people.

According to documents at the Public Record Office for the years 1697-8 (Customs 3/1, part 2, Export), English clocks and watches were then exported to Denmark, Sweden, Flanders, Germany, Holland, Italy, Russia, Turkey, Barbados, New England and Pennsylvania. On English exports in general cf. also SAVARY, *Dictionnaire*, vol. 3, col. 329-42. For English exports to Turkey cf. BRITTEN, *Old Clocks*, pp. 95-6 and 166. On exports of English and Swiss time-pieces to China cf. below the following chapter.

5 In 1786 a conference was held in London at which questions relating to clocks and watches trade were fully debated and answers thereto agreed upon as follows (ATKINS and OVER-ALL, *Company of Clockmakers*, p. 263): . . . *Question*: 'To what Countries do you (watch and clockmakers) now export Clocks and Watches?' *Answer*: 'We export clocks and watches to all commercial countries except France; and particularly to Holland, Flanders, Germany, Sweden, Denmark, Norway, Russia, Spain, Portugal, Italy, Turkey, East and West Indies, China, etc.' . . . *Question*: 'In what does the export of watches chiefly consist, in those of Gold, Silver or Metal and to what Countries are they exported respectively?' *Answer*: 'To East India, chiefly gold, to China, chiefly metal, to Holland, many gold, few metal and a great many silver; to other Countries, some of each, principally silver, though to Spain, a great many valuable gold watches accompany the silver ones' . . . *Question*: 'What number of watches do you conceive to be the whole of the exports to different parts of the World?'

Answer: 'It is very difficult to determine the number of watches exported from this Country, but by the nearest calculation we are able to make we presume about eighty thousand per annum' . . . Question: 'Are there many French watches brought into this Country?' *Answer*: 'Great quantities of gold watches very detrimental to the manufacture of this Kingdom, which numbers are greatly increased by the late duty of eight shillings per oz. on wrought gold plate.' On the number of clocks and watches produced in Clerkenwell, cf. GEORGE, *London Life*, p. 174.

6 CHAPUISAT, *Commerce et industrie à Geneve*, p. 217, who derives his data from Sismondi. A French report written by two clockmakers brings the figure to 250,000 watches, but it was an obvious exaggeration (BABEL, *Histoire corporative de l'horlogerie*, p. 398. Cf. also BABEL, *Fabrique genevoise*, pp. 51-2, and SAY, *Economie Politique*, vol. 1, p. 187).

7 On the story of Western timepieces on the Turkish market see Kurz, *European Clocks and Watches in the Near East*. This remarkable book not only provides information on a fascinating chapter in the history of Western technology but it also illuminates Eastern mental attitudes and the intriguing problem of relations between the West and the Near Eastern world.

NOTES TO CHAPTER II

PAGE 76

1 BOXER, *Portuguese in the East*, pp. 192 and 214.
2 CIPOLLA, *Guns and Sails*, pp. 138ff.

PAGE 77

1 From 1565 to 1815 Spanish galleons regularly made the five-to-eight month voyage across the Pacific between Manila and Acapulco. The galleons carried to the Philippines silver and returned to Mexico laden with Asian products. Cf. SCHURZ, *The Manila Galleon*.

PAGE 78

1 VAN LINSCHOTEN, *Voyage to the East Indies*, vol. 1, p. 10.
2 CARLETTI, *My Voyage around the World*, p. 153. The report by Carletti was addressed to the Archduke of Florence. Carletti obviously referred to the '*scudi d'oro*' (cf. *ibid.*, p. 144) which were in his days the main gold currency of Florence. A Florentine '*scudo*' was worth slightly more than three grams of pure gold. Thus, according to Carletti, 'Portugal and Spain alone' brought into China every year an amount of silver roughly equivalent to about 4.5 metric tons of gold.

3 Cf. MORSE, *East India Company*, vol. 1, pp. 8, 307-13 and *passim*; CHAUDHURI, *East India Company*, pp. 24-5; and DERMIGNY, *Le Commerce à Canton*, vol. 2, pp. 687-767.

4 DERMIGNY, *Le Commerce à Canton*, vol. 2, pp. 724*ff.*

5 MORSE, *East India Company*, vol. 1, p. 67.

PAGE 79

1 MORSE, *East India Company*, vol. 1, p. 109.

2 For all that precedes cf. PANIKKAR, *Asia and Western Dominance*, p. 53. Indonesians, Chinese and Japanese showed little interest in Western art, but Indian and Persian potentates often asked for Western artists and paintings. Cf. BOXER, *The Dutch Seaborne Empire*, p. 172.

3 MORSE, *East India Company*, vol. 1, p. 114.

4 CARY, *Discourse on Trade*, p. 43. CHAUDHURI, *East India Company*, p. 29, quotes reports by the Company's factors in India, Japan and Persia, who complained that the English cloth was too highly priced for local buyers. The higher cost of labour in Europe made European manufactures scarcely competitive with Asian products.

PAGE 80

1 Cf. among others THOMAS, *Mercantilism and the East India Trade*, especially pp. 118*ff.*

2 WEBER, *Compagnie Française des Indes*, pp. 234-5; DERMIGNY, *Le Commerce à Canton*, vol. 1, pp. 196*ff.*

3 DERMIGNY, *Le Commerce à Canton*, vol. 1, p. 196.

4 D'ELIA, *Fonti Ricciane*, vol. 1, p. 33. NIEUHOFF, *Embassy to China* at p. 166 follows almost literally the description by Ricci but at p. 227 he adds: 'upon the clock-house Turrets stands an instrument which shows the hour of the day by means of water, which running from one vessel into another raises a board, upon which is portrayed a mark for the time of the day; and you are to observe that there is always one remaining there, to take notice of the passing of the time, who at every hour signifies the same to the people by beating upon a drum and hanging out a board with the hour writ upon it in large letters'. Cf. also PIERRE DE GOYA and JACOB DE KEYSER quoted by CHAPUIS, *Montre Chinoise*, p. 15, and

LE COMTE, *Empire of China*, p. 81, NEEDHAM, *Heavenly Clockwork*, pp. 155ff, and *Science and Civilization in China*, vol. 4, part 2, pp. 437ff criticizes the opinion of Ricci and emphasizes the fact that centuries before the arrival of the Portuguese the Chinese had built the 'heavenly clockwork'. But Prof. Needham fails to demonstrate that there is room for reasonable comparison between the 'heavenly clockwork' and the Western mechanical clocks, and on the other hand he is forced to admit (p. 156) that Chinese horological skills 'perished in the wave of Confucian austerity which accompanied the rise to power of the nationalist dynasty of the Ming.' To maintain that the Western clock was not a novelty in China because of the monumental striking water-wheel clock made at the time of the last Yuan emperor is just like maintaining that Watt's engine was not a novelty in Europe because of the gadgets devised by Heron in classical times.

Unexpected support for Professor Needham's view may be found in an anonymous work published in Geneva in 1689 (*L'excellence de l'horlogerie*, pp. 14-15), which fantastically credits the Chinese with the invention of the 'portable watch'. On the Eastern 'clocks' that made use of incense to measure time cf. BEDINI, *The Scent of Time*.

PAGE 81

1   D'ELIA, *Fonti Ricciane*, vol. 1, pp. 161-7.

PAGE 82

1   D'ELIA, *Fonti Ricciane*, vol. 1, p. 192.
2   D'ELIA, *Fonti Ricciane*, vol. 1, pp. 201-12.

PAGE 83

1   D'ELIA, *Fonti Ricciane*, vol. 2, p. 123 *n.* 7, and p. 124, *n.* 1.
2   On the clocks and the activity of the Jesuits in China, cf. ENSHOFF, *Ricci's Uhren*, pp. 190-4; SARREIRA, *Horas boas e*

horas mas, pp. 518-28; BETTRAY, *Akkomodationmethode des P. Matteo Ricci,* pp. 26-32, 107, 114, 118, 120 and 171; LAMALLE, *La propagande du P. Nicolas Trigault,* pp. 75, 101, *n.* 34 and *passim.*

The views of Enshoff and Sarreira about the 'unequal hours' in China have been convincingly criticized by D'ELIA, *Fonti Ricciane,* vol. 2, p. 128, *n.* 5.

3 D'ELIA, *Fonti Ricciane,* vol. 2, pp. 120-8.

PAGE 86

1 On the workshop established at the Imperial Palace by Emperor K'ang Hsi cf. CHAPUIS, *Montre Chinoise,* pp. 42-4; PLANCHON, *L'Horloge,* chap. 10, and BEDINI, *Chinese Mechanical Clocks,* pp. 213-4. Harcourt-Smith (*Catalogue,* p. 2), who studied the Imperial collection of clocks in the 1930's, writes that 'with the exception of about six pieces, all the clocks and watches which I have been able to examine in the two museums are of a date subsequent to 1760; no traces can be found of Matteo Ricci's clocks or of the pieces committed by K'ang Hsi to the care of Father Stadlin'. In the collection of M. E. Gélis in Paris there was, however, a clock that had been made in the Imperial workshop either in the last years of Emperor K'ang Hsi or in the early years of his successor Yung Cheng (1723-1735): for a description of this piece cf. CHAPUIS, *Montre Chinoise,* p. 43, and for its dating *ibid.,* *n.* 1. In MONREAL Y TEJADA, *Relojes antiguos,* no. 87, cf. the description of another clock that was made in China toward the end of the eighteenth century and that had been erroneously attributed to European clockmakers because of its similarity with contemporary clocks made in Europe.

According to PLANCHON, *L'horloge,* chap. 10, the time-pieces produced at the Imperial workshop were very crude replicas of European specimens (cf. also BEDINI, *Chinese Mechanical Clocks,* pp. 218-19). On the work done at the Imperial workshop cf. also *Instructions sublimes et familiares de Cheng-Tzu-Quogen-Hoang-Ti,* p. 179. (Cheng Tsu Jen

Huang Ti is the temple name of Emperor K'ang Hsi.) In this text the Emperor emphasizes that the Chinese craftsmen encountered the greatest difficulty in the making of springs, 'but I succeeded in getting from the Europeans the know-how for making such springs and I was able to have made hundreds and thousands of clocks that are very good time-keepers'.

2   On Father François-Louis Stadlin (1658-1740) cf. CHAPUIS, *Montre Chinoise*, p. 45, and PFISTER, *Notices biographiques*, pp. 619-20.

3   On Father Valentin Chalier (1697-1747), cf. PFISTER, *Notices biographiques*, pp. 718-20.

4   PELLIOT, *Bulletin Critique*, p. 66. The statement by Father Chalier seems to contradict Harcourt-Smith, *Catalogue*, p. 2, who writes that 'contrary to popular belief, hardly any of the pieces herein described are of French workmanship'. However, one has to consider that Harcourt-Smith saw only what remained of the fabulous Imperial collection after the looting of Yuan-Ming Yuan in 1860, that of the Forbidden City in 1900 and the troubles of the early twentieth century. On the Imperial Collection cf. also CHAPUIS, *Montre Chinoise*, pp. 27-9.

5   PELLIOT, *Bulletin Critique*, p. 66.

PAGE 87

1   HARCOURT-SMITH, *Catalogue*, p. 1.

2   D'ELIA, *Fonti Ricciane*, vol. 1, p. 252 and 259. According to PFISTER, *Notices biographiques*, p. 29, n. 1, Father Mathew Ricci's repute was very great among Chinese clockmakers still in the early twentieth century and 'in the shops of many a clockmaker in Shanghai Matteo Ricci is honoured as the saint protector of the craft'.

3   VERBIEST, *Astronomia Europaea*, section Horolotechnia.

4   The Chinese built astronomical clockworks centuries before the European made the first mechanical clocks. This, however, does not contradict what is said above in the text. I am not suggesting that the Chinese did not try to conceive

contrivances for measuring the time or simulating the movements of the heavens. I submit that foreign machinery could not be properly appreciated because it was not the expression of a Chinese response to problems set by a Chinese environment.

5 Cf. the brilliant remarks by DERMIGNY, *Le Commerce à Canton*, vol. 1, p. 47. When Emperor K'ang Hsi wrote the 'sublime instructions' for his children, he referred to the mechanical timepieces of Western type as to beautiful and expensive toys. Emperor K'ang Hsi established a workshop for the making and mending of clocks and watches at the Imperial Palace in Peking. He seems to have attached great importance to the fact that he succeeded in having good mechanical timepieces made at his workshop; yet he writes to his children 'do not you think you are very fortunate? Because of my initiative, you can play with ten or twenty self-ringing-bells'. Cf. *Instructions sublimes et familiares de Cheng-Tzu-Quogen-Hoang Ti*, p. 179.

PAGE 88

1 CARLETTI, *Voyage around the world*, p. 153. One may re-remember here that a 'triangular-shaped glass' of the kind described by Carletti and of Venetian manufacture was among the presents offered by the Jesuits to the Viceroy of Kwantung in 1582: cf. D'ELIA, *Fonti Ricciane*, vol. 1, p. 166.
2 D'ELIA, *Fonti Ricciane*, vol. 1, p. 42.
3 CHIANG, *Tides from the West*, pp. 34-5. Still at the end of the nineteenth century, J. D. BALL, *Things Chinese*, p. 709, wrote that 'at the Treaty Ports and in their neighbourhood, as well as at Hong Kong and Macao, clocks are found in every shop and watches abound, but in many places there is no standard of correct time, and in places where there is, it is ignored extensively'.

PAGE 89

1 About the end of the eighteenth century, Van Braam

(*Account of the Embassy*) gave a different explanation of the attitude of the Chinese toward Western machinery.

He wrote that (vol. 1, p. 242) the Chinese 'think that they hold the first rank among all the created beings of this immense universe', and that they are 'the first nation to be found throughout the vast extent of space . . .' (vol. 1, p. 243) 'It may be perhaps supposed that the sight of the masterpieces of art, which the Chinese receive annually from Europe, will open their eyes and convince them that industry is there carried farther than among themselves, and that our genius surpasses theirs; but their vanity finds a remedy for this. All these wonders are included in the class of super-fluities, and by placing them beneath their wants, they place them at the same time beneath their regard. If, for a moment, they fall into an involuntary fit of astonishment, they come out of it firmly resolved to do nothing to imitate that by which it was produced.'

2 *Ssu—K'u ch'üan-shu ti-yao*, vol. 55, Tze—pu, sect. 7, p. 5.

3 PFISTER, *Notices biographiques*, p. 914.

PAGE 90

1 VAN BRAAM, *Account of the Embassy*, vol. 2, pp. 47-8.

2 DE GUIGNES, *Voyages à Peking*, vol. 1, p. 425.

3 ABEL, *Journey to the Interior of China*, p. 82 *n.*

4 ROBERTSON, *Evolution of Clockwork*, p. 196.

PAGE 91

1 CHAPUIS, *Montre Chinoise*, pp. 46-50; CHAPUIS and DROZ, *Automata*, pp. 77-84. The 'last Dutch Embassy to the Chinese Court' (1794-5) led by Van Braam presented the Emperor with two most ingenious timepieces the description of which fills three and a half pages in Van Braam's report (appendix G). The *Ta—Ch'ing Hui-Tien Shih—li*, chap. 394, p. 6, describes one of the pieces as follows: 'a musical clock that wishes happiness for 10,000 years with chimes every quarter of an hour'. A memorandum to the Emperor from

156

Chün-chi-ch'u (Jan. 1795) says 'conforming (to instructions) we have carefully compared the list of tribute-articles now presented by the country of Holland and the list of articles recently presented by the country of England. We find that there were in all six large instruments presented by the country of England while now the country of Holland has merely one pair of musical clocks and four pairs of gold watches' (for all this cf. DUYVENDAK, *The Last Dutch Embassy*, pp. 59-60, and DUYVENDAK, *Supplementary documents*, p. 345).

2 An interesting episode was related by Van Braam (*Account of the Embassy*, vol. 2, p. 20) at the end of the eighteenth century: '[The *Voo-Tchong-Tang*] sent us his watch, desiring us to let him know what we thought of it. As it was made by Arnold, we had it in our power to praise it without flattery. The *Voo-Tchong-Tang* then desired to see ours, and afterwards spoke of the high price of some watches in the possession of our mechanist, which he said he should be glad to buy at an easier rate, observing at the same time that his only cost him three hundred and seventy-five *livres*. It would have been easy for us to give him a very intelligible explanation of this low price; but the fear of the consequences that might have attended it in respect to the transactions of the mandarins and merchants of Canton, and particularly the risk that might be run by the former, prevented me from going into particulars; and we contented ourselves with expressing our surprise at such a watch being procured for so small a sum . . . ; (p. 23) From the tenor of the *Voo-Tchong-Tang's* discourse this morning, I see plainly that the Court is not acquainted with the underhand dealings of the mandarins at Canton. . . . It is certain that even in London Arnold never sold a watch for 375 *livres* and that no Chinese merchant could be able to procure one at Canton for less than six or eight times that sum'.

3 D'ELIA, *Fonti Ricciane*, vol. 1, p. 382.

PAGE 92

1 BARROW, *Travels in China*, p. 231.
2 The information regarding the Court Minutes and the China Factory Records were kindly supplied to me by the Assistant Keeper of the India Office Records. I owe the information regarding the English Custom books to Miss A. M. Millard, who searched for me Customs 3/1 part 2 Exports and Customs 2/5 and 2/6 at the Public Record Office in London.
3 This information was kindly given to me by Miss E. J. Karreman, who consulted for me the 'Invoices of incoming and outgoing cargoes no. 762-816' and the 'Accounts of the money expended on the Journey to Edo and on gifts for Japanese authorities 1642/3-1818' no. 1161-1305 p. 56 in the *Archive of the Dutch factory in Japan* at The Hague.
4 DUHALDE, *General History of China*, vol. 2, p. 302.
5 The statement that clocks and watches were in Canton 'as cheap as in Europe' seems highly exaggerated. For prices of Western clocks sold in China at the end of the eighteenth century cf. DE GUIGNES, *Voyages à Peking*, vol. 3, p. 271.

PAGE 93

1 Cf. CHAPUIS, *Montre Chinoise*, pp. 25*ff* and 51*ff*; NEEDHAM, *Heavenly Clockwork*, pp. 150-4; and DERMIGNY, *Le commerce à Canton*, vol. 3, pp. 1237*ff*. In the nineteenth century it was remarked that 'preference is given in China to English watches because they are the only ones that the clockmakers in Canton are able to repair' (DOBEL, *Sept années en Chine*, p. 30).
2 DERMIGNY, *Le commerce à Canton*, vol. 3, p. 1239 and p. 1240 *n*. 1.
3 Cf. among others HARCOURT-SMITH, *Catalogue*; CHAPUIS *Montre Chinoise*; CHAPUIS and DROZ, *Automata*, pp. 107-18.
4 *Notice sur les objets de commerce à importer en Chine*, p. 270.
5 OSBECK, *Voyage to China and the East Indies*, vol. 1, p. 236.

PAGE 94

1 BARROW, *Travels in China*, p. 181.
2 BROWN, *The Impact of fire-arms*, pp. 236-53.

PAGE 95

1 ROBERTSON, *Evolution of Clockwork*, pp. 276-7.
2 It should be added that while in European timepieces hours were struck in ascending progression from 1 to 12, in Japan the hours were traditionally marked by strokes on the temple bells in descending order from 9 to 4. Cf. ROBERTSON, *Evolution of Clockwork*, p. 197.
3 ROBERTSON, *Evolution of Clockwork*, p. 197.
4 TSUKADA, *Wadokei*, p. 37; TAKABASHI, *Tokei Hattatzu shi*, pp. 47-8.
5 For all that precedes cf. ROBERTSON, *Evolution of Clockwork*, pp. 219-26, and 240-3. MONREAL y TEJADA, *Relojes Antiguos* (p. 17 of the Introduction) writes that '*el Japón conservó su hora antigua y tradiciónal hasta la segunda mitad del siglo pasado y los relojeros de Europa—principalmente lôs holandeses que fueron los primeros en comerciar con aquel país—hubieron de ingeniarse para adaptar sus maquinarias al complicado cómputo oriental*'. He therefore implies that the peculiar mechanical characteristics of the *Wadokei* were the product not of Japanese ingenuity but of European—and probably Dutch —clockmakers eager to sell timepieces on the Japanese market. There is no evidence, however, to support this thesis. The evidence available about the export of Dutch clocks to Japan (cf. above note 3 to p. 92) seems actually to contradict Senor Monreal y Tejada's views, although we cannot exclude *a priori* the possibility that some European clockmaker might have been working in Japan before the 1630's (ROBERTSON, *Evolution of Clockwork*, p. 197).

PAGE 96

1 All clocks made in Japan in the course of the seventeenth

and eighteenth centuries were weight-driven. Spring-driven clocks were first made in the 1830's (ROBERTSON, *Evolution of Clockwork*, p. 247). The reason for the late appearance of the spring-driven clocks must have resided in the difficulty of producing springs. In China, Emperor K'ang Hsi in his 'sublime instructions' (cf. above note 1 to p. 86) mentions that craftsmen at the Imperial workshop had great difficulties in producing springs for clocks and watches. At the end of the eighteenth century, Barrow (*Travels in China*, p. 306) reported that the Chinese 'discover no want of genius to conceive nor of dexterity to execute and their imitative powers have always been acknowledged to be very great . . . a Chinese in Canton on being shewn an European watch undertook, and succeeded, to make one like it, though he had never seen anything of the kind before, but it was necessary to furnish him with a main spring, which he could not make'.

2 TAKABASHI, *Tokei Hattatzu shi*, p. 55; TSUKADA, *Wadokei*, p. 66.

3 TSUKADA, *Wadokei*, p. 70. Cf. also below note 2 to p. 98.

PAGE 97

1 In an effort to improve the finances of the *shōgun*, in 1710 Arai Hakuseki allegedly discharged over fifty people who attended the clocks in the clocks' room at Edo Castle. Regrettably enough we are not informed about the number of clocks then existing in the castle. Cf. TSUKADA, *Wadokei*, pp. 33-4.

2 Cf. the passage by father J. R. Tcuzu quoted by BEDINI, *The Scent of Time*, p. 34.

3 A Japanese clockmaker made all parts of a timepiece and specialization among craftsmen in regard to the production of single parts of timepieces did not develop in old Japan. There was no standardization of production and one can hardly find two old '*wadokei*' that look identical. It is generally believed that it took more than one year for a craftsman to produce a clock and it is said that some of the

famous makers produced less than ten clocks during their lifetime. Cf. TSUKADA, *Wadokei*, p. 15 and *passim*.

4   Also abroad the Chinese failed to develop clock manufactures. At the end of the seventeenth century FRYKE, *Relation of a voyage*, p. 28, wrote that at 'Batavia the inhabitants are of all nations as Amboineses, Malabarians, Mardigarians, etc., but the Chinese are the chief and greater part. . . . They (the Chinese) exceed all the others by far in cunning and policy, and are very good mechanicks; and there are of them of all trades excepting clock-work or watch-work'.

5   OSBECK, *Voyage to China and the East Indies*, vol. 1, p. 236.

6   PFISTER, *Notices Biographiques*, p. 914.

7   DERMIGNY, *Le commerce à Canton*, vol. 3, p. 1239.

8   VAN BRAAM, *Account of the Embassy*, vol. 2, pp. 212-13. Van Braam (*ibid.*, vol. 1, p. 204) also relates that the two elaborate clocks that were to be given as presents to the Emperor suffered some damage during the transportation. When the Embassy arrived in Peking 'three Chinese watch-makers in the service of the Court came to see if it would be possible to mend them in a few days, under the direction of our mechanist, but the latter declared that as he could not make them understand him, it was impossible for them to be employed'. In Peking there were no craftsmen capable of mending an elaborate clock at the end of the eighteenth century, but in Canton the situation was somewhat better. M. De Guignes (*Voyages à Peking*, vol. 2, p. 1) referring to the same episode related by Van Braam, wrote that '*vu qu'ils n'avôient personne* (in Peking) *en état de le fair* (to mend the clock), *on devoit l'envoyer à Quanton pour la reparer*'. Again at the end of the eighteenth century Barrow (*Travels in China*, p. 306) remarked that the Chinese 'now fabricate in Canton as well as in London, and at one third of the expence, all those ingenious pieces of mechanism which at one time were sent to China in such vast quantities from the repositories of Coxe and Merlin'.

9   Cf. previous note.

1 CIPOLLA, *Guns and Sails*, pp. 116-27.

2 According to TAKABASHI, *Tokei Hattatzu shi*, p. 52, clocks were regarded as oddities.   In the eighteenth century, according to a Japanese book on horology, mechanical clocks were owned only by 'noblemen, rich merchants and collectors of curiosities' (*ibid.*, p. 51).

3 On a Chinese silk tapestry, in the National Maritime Museum, Greenwich, one sees a representation of the bringing of clocks and astronomical instruments as gifts by the Embassy of Lord Macartney (1793 A.D.).   In the upper right-hand corner one reads the following proud and chauvinistic inscription:

> *Strange things we prize not, nor do we listen to boastful claims*
>
> *yet mindful of the great distance journeyed, we shall repay a hundredfold.*

At the end of the eighteenth century, Barrow (*Travels in China*, p. 306) was aware of 'the pride or the policy of the (Chinese) government affecting to despise anything new or foreign'.   Cf. also the passage by Van Braam quoted above, footnote 1 to p. 89.

4   Cf. above note 1 to p. 86.

5 On the contrasting performance of the Japanese and the Chinese cf. BEDINI, *Chinese Mechanical Clocks*, p. 218.

6 BILFINGER, *Die Mittelalterlichen Horen.*

7 NEEDHAM, *Heavenly Clockwork*, p. 201.

8 In China the full cycle of twelve equal double-hours is found stabilized in the Han period (from the beginning of the second century B.C. onward) but it probably goes well back into the Chou period (NEEDHAM, *Heavenly Clockwork*, pp. 201*ff*).

9 NEEDHAM, *Heavenly Clockwork*, pp. 199-202, and DE SAUSSURE, *L'horometrie et le système cosmologique des Chinois* in CHAPUIS, *Montre Chinoise*, pp. 1-18.

PAGE 99

1   BRUSONI, *Varie osservazioni*, p. 13.
2   Cf. LUZZATTO, *Girolamo Brusoni* (1899), pp. 237-8.
3   D'ELIA, *Fonti Ricciane*, vol. I, p. 29. In 1736 Father Chalier referred to the craftsmen who worked under him at the Imperial workshop as to '*ouvriers esclaves*', i.e. 'slave workers' (PELLIOT, *Bulletin Critique*, p. 66). The term 'slave' however, was probably used by Father Chalier in a rather loose sense (on the general question of the slave-craftsmen in China, cf. NEEDHAM, *Science and Civilization*, vol. 4, part 2, pp. 23*ff*). According to a custom developed during the Ming dynasty, Chinese craftsmen could be recruited by the State and compelled to meet the needs of the Imperial government at relatively low pay. Father Chalier probably referred to this type of forced labour. On this system of compulsory service cf. HO, *Ladder of Success*, pp. 56-7.

PAGE 100

1   PRODAN, *Chinese Art*, p. 26.
2   FRIESE, *Zum Aufstieg von Handwerken*, pp. 161-72 noticed that it is very difficult to compile biographies of Chinese artisans. This alone indicates how strongly the 'gentry' opposed the entry into its ranks of people who lacked the qualification based on state examinations. Such people were simply ignored. NEEDHAM, *Poverty and Triumphs*, pp. 130-1, referring to the life of Ma Chün, an ingenious technician and inventor of the thirteenth century, notices that 'Ma Chün was quite incapable of arguing with the sophisticated scholars nursed in the classical literary traditions, and in spite of all the efforts of his admirers, could never attain any position of importance in the service of the state or even the means to prove by practical test the value of the inventions which he made'. On the whole question cf. also the important remarks by HO, *The Ladder of Success*, pp. 41*ff* and 56*ff*.

3 For instances of favours bestowed on Japanese clockmakers by Japanese lords cf. TSUKADA, *Wadokei*, pp. 67 and 69; BONJINSHA, *Daijinmei Jiten*, p. 67. In China on the contrary, as Barrow clearly saw (*Travels in China*, p. 306), 'the general want of encouragement to new inventions, however ingenious, has been greatly detrimental to the progress of arts and manufactures'.

4 In reporting that Mao ven lung used Dutch guns against the invading Manchus NIEUHOFF, *Embassy to China*, p. 296, remarks that Mao 'was native of the province of Quantung where he had learned and understood in his conversation among the Portuguese in Macao several things concerning military discipline'. At the end of the eighteenth century, Barrow (*Travels in China*, p. 306) noticed that the Chinese 'now fabricate in Canton as well as in London, and at one third of the expence' clocks and watches. On the other hand, conservatism was particularly strong in the interior provinces where still at the middle of the nineteenth century most of the governors resisted any innovation and especially the adoption of Western ideas and techniques (CHEN, *Lin Tse-hsü*, pp. 58-60).

5 NIEUHOFF, *Embassy to China*, p. 166.

PAGE 101

1 HO, *Population of China*, pp. 264-70.

2 TAEUBER, *Population of Japan*, p. 20.

3 CRAWFURD, *Indian Archipelago*, p. 525, pointed out that China's sea-coast is very limited in relation to the vast area of the country.

4 SHELDON, *Rise of the merchant class in Tokugawa Japan*.

5 Cf. DERMIGNY, *Commerce à Canton*, vol. 1, pp. 63 and 69.

NOTES TO THE EPILOGUE

PAGE 104

1 The best work available on the subject is still BILFINGER,
   Die Mittelalterlichen Horen. In addition one may consult
   also FRANKLIN, *Mésure du temps*, pp. 63*ff*; USHER, *Mechanical
   inventions*, p. 208; LE GOFF, *Le temps du travail*, pp. 597*ff*;
   LE GOFF, *Temps de l'Eglise et temps du marchand*, pp. 424*ff*;
   FASANO-GUARINI, *Comment naviguent les galères*, pp. 281-2.
2 PEATE, *Clock and watchmakers*, p. 14.
3 FRANKLIN, *Mésure du temps*, p. 139.

PAGE 105

1 FROISSART, *Li Orloge amoureuses*.
2 RENIER, *Gaspare Visconti*, pp. 541-2.
3 ROSSI, *I filosofi e le macchine*, pp. 143-5. According to WHITE,
   Medieval Technology, p. 125, it is in the works of Nicolas
   Oresmus (*d.* A.D. 1382) that we first find the metaphor of the
   Universe as a vast mechanical clock created and set running
   by God so that 'all the wheels move as harmoniously as
   possible'.
4 SCITOVSKY, *Papers*, pp. 219*ff*.
5 DE SAINT EXUPÉRY, *Wind, Sand and Stars*, pp. 71-2.

BIBLIOGRAPHY

ABEL, C., *Narrative of a Journey in the interior of China (1816-17)*. London, 1818.

Annali della Fabbrica del Duomo, Milan, 1877.

ATKINS, S. E., and W. H. OVERALL, *Some Account of the Worshipful Company of Clockmakers of the City of London*. London, 1881.

ATTON, H., and H. H. HOLLAND, *The King's Customs*. London, 1908.

BABEL, A., *Histoire corporative de l'horlogerie, de l'orfèvrerie et des industries annexes*, in 'Mémoires et Documents publiés par la Société d'Histoire et d'Archéologie de Genève, vol. 33, Geneva, 1916.

BABEL, A., Les premiers horlogers genevois in *Journal Suisse d'horlogerie*, 2 (1921), pp. 34-7.

BABEL, A., L'horlogerie genevoise á Constantinople et dans le Levant du XVIme au XVIIIme siècle, in *Etrennes genevoises*, 1927 (1926), pp. 61-74.

BABEL, A., Un horloger genevois du XVIme siècle, Charles Cusin, in *Le Collaborateur*, 12 (1930), pp. 1-4.

BABEL, A., *La fabrique genevoise*. Neuchatel—Paris, 1938

BABEL, A., Les foires d'autresfois et les horlogers de Genève in *Journal Suisse des horlogers*, (April 1943), pp. 29-30.

BABEL, A., *Histoire écononomique de Genève*. Genève, 1963.

BABINGER, F., Maometto II il Conquistatore e l'Italia, in *Rivista Storica Italiana*, 63 (1951), pp. 469-505.

BAILLIE, G. H., *Watchmakers and Clockmakers of the World*. London, 1929.

BALL, J. D., *Things Chinese*. Hong Kong, 1903.

BARBIERI, G., I redditi dei milanesi all'inizio della dominazione spagnola, in *Rivista Internazionale di Scienze Sociali*, 45 (1937), pp. 759-81.

BIBLIOGRAPHY

BARROW, J., *Travels in China*. London 1804.

von BASSERMANN-JORDAN, E., *Uhren* (ed. H. von Bertele). Brunswick, 1961.

BATTARA, P., *La popolazione di Firenze alla metà del 1500*. Florence, 1935.

BAVOUX, E., *Voltaire à Ferney. Sa correspondance avec la duchesse de Saxe-Gotha*. Paris, 1865.

BEDINI, S. A., Chinese mechanical clocks in *Bulletin of the National Association of Watch and Clock Collectors*, 7 (1956), p. 211-21.

BEDINI, S. A., *Johann Philipp Treffler Clockmaker of Augsburg*. Columbia, 1956.

BEDINI, S. A., Agent for the Archduke. Another chapter in the story of Johann Philipp Treffler, clockmaker of Augsburg, in *Physis*, 3 (1961), pp. 137-58.

BEDINA, S. A., The Scent of time, in *Transactions of the American Philosophical Society* N. S. vol. 53, part 5. Philadelphia, 1963.

BEILLARD, A., *Recherches sur l'Horlogerie*. Paris, 1895.

BELGRANO, L. T., Degli antichi orologi pubblici d'Italia con aggiunte e notizie della Posta in Genova, in *Archivio Storico Italiano*, 7 (1868), pp. 28-68.

BELTRAMI, D., *Storia della popolazione di Venezia dalla fine del secolo XVI alla caduta della Repubblica*. Padova, 1954.

BEN-DAVID, J., Scientific Growth: a sociological view, in *Minerva* (1964), pp. 455-76.

BERGIER, J. F. and L. SOLARI, Histoire et élaboration statistique. L'exemple de la population de Genève au XVe siècle, in *Mélanges d'histoire économique et sociale en hommage au professeur Antony Babel*, Geneva, 1963, vol. 1, pp. 197-225.

von BERTELE, H., Precision Time-keeping in the pre-Huygens Era, in *Horological Journal*, 95 (1953), p. 794-816.

BERTOLOTTI, A., Le Arti minori alla Corte di Mantova nei secoli XV, XVI e XVII, in *Archivio Storico Lombardo*, 15 (1888), pp. 259-318 and 419-590.

BETTRAY, J., *Die Akkomodationsmethode des P. Matteo Ricci S.J. in China*. Rome, 1955.

BIANQUIS, J., *La Révocation de l'Édit de Nantes à Rouen*. Rouen, 1885.

BILFINGER, G., *Der Bürgerliche Tag*, Stuttgart, 1888.

BILFINGER, G., *Die Mittelalterlichen Horen und die Modernen Stunden. Ein Beitrag zur Kulturgeschichte*. Stuttgart, 1892.

BONJINSHA, (ed.), *Daijinmei Jiten*. Tokyo, 1955.

BONNANT, G., The Introduction of Western Horology in China, in *La Suisse Horlogère* , I (1960), pp. 28-38.

BORCHARDT, L., *Die altägyptische Zeitmessung*. Berlin, 1920.

DU BOURG, A., Coup d'oeil historique sur les diverses corporations de Toulouse, in *Mémoires de la Société Archéologique du Midi de la France*, 13 (1883-5), pp. 257-96; 14 (1886-89), pp. 52-103.

BOURRIAU, R. P., *Notes pour servir à l'histoire des horlogers à la Rochelle du XVIe siècle au début du XVIIIe siècle*. Besançon 1934.

BOXER, C. R., The Portuguese in the East, in *Portugal and Brazil*, ed. by H. V. Livermore. Oxford, 1953.

BOXER, C. R., *The Dutch seaborne Empire 1500-1800*. London, 1965.

BOYLE, R., *Works*. London, 1772.

VAN BRAAM, A. E., *An authentic account of the Embassy of the Dutch East India Company*. London 1798.

BRETT, G., The Automata in the Byzantine Throne of Solomon, in *Speculum*, 29 (1954), pp. 477-87.

BRING, S. E., A contribution to the biography of Christopher Polhem, in *Christopher Polhem, the father of Swedish Technology*. Hartford, Conn. 1963.

BRITTEN, F. J., *Old clocks and watches and their makers* (7th edn. ed. and revised by G.H. Baillie, C. Clutton and C. A. Ilbert). New York, 1956.

BROWN, D. M., The impact of fire-arms on Japanese warfare, in *The Far Eastern Quarterly*, 7 (1948), pp. 236-53.

BROWN, H., *Scientific Organizations in Seventeenth Century France*. Baltimore, 1934.

BRUNE, P., *Dictionnaire des Artistes et ouvriers d'art de la Franche-Comté*. Paris, 1912.

BRUSONI, G., *Varie osservationi sopra le Relazioni Universali di G. Botero*. Venice, 1659.

BRUTON, E., *Dictionary of Clocks and Watches*. New York, 1963.
168

CAFFI, M., Il Castello di Pavia, in *Archivio Storico Lombardo*, 3 (1876), pp. 543-59.

CAMPORI, G., Gli orologieri degli Estensi, in *Atti e Memorie delle RR. Deputazioni di Storia Patria per le Provincie dell'Emilia*, N.S., vol. 2 (1877), pp. 243-65.

CANETTA, C., Vicende edilizie del Castello di Milano, in *Archivio Storico Lombardo*, 10 (1883), pp. 327-80.

CARLETTI, F., *My voyage around the world* (ed. H. Weinstock). New York, 1964.

CARSTEN, F. L., Medieval Democracy in the Brandenburg Towns and its defeat in the fifteenth century, in *Change in Medieval Society* (ed. S. L. Thrupp), New York, 1964, pp. 297-313.

CARY, J., *A discourse on trade and other matters relative to it*. London, 1745.

CAUSSY, F., *Voltaire, Seigneur de Village*. Paris, 1912.

CHAPUIS, A. (with the collaboration of G. Loup and L. de Saussure), *La Montre Chinoise*. Neuchatel 1919.

CHAPUIS, A., Voltaire horloger, Catherine II et la Chine. in *Hora*, July 1921. ·

CHAPUIS, A., *Le Grand Frédéric et ses horlogers*. Lausanne, 1938.

CHAUPUIS, A., and GELIS, *Le Monde des Automates*. Paris, 1928.

CHAPUIS, A., and E. DROZ, *Automata: a Historical and Technological Study*. Neuchatel-London, 1958.

CHAPUISAT, E., *Le commerce et l'industrie à Genève pendant la domination française*. Geneva-Paris, 1908.

CHAUDHURI, K. N., The East India Company and the Export of Treasure in the Early Seventeenth Century, in *The Economic History Review*, 16 (1963), pp. 23-38.

CHEN, G., *Lin Tse-Hsü*. Peiping, 1934.

CHIANG, M., *Tides from the West*. New Haven, 1947.

CHIU, Kai-ming, The Introduction of spectacles into China, in *Harvard Journal of Asiatic Studies* (1936), pp. 186-93.

CIPOLLA, C. M., The Decline of Italy, in *The Economic History Review*, second series, 5 (1952), pp. 178-87.

CIPOLLA, C. M., *Guns and Sails in the early phase of European Expansion*. London, 1965.

Codex Carolinus seu volumen Epistolarum, in *Recueil des*

Historiens des Gaules et de la France, vol. 5 (Paris, 1869), pp. 485-636.

CRAWFURD, J., *History of the Indian Archipelago*. London-Edinburgh, 1820.

CROMBIE, A. C., *Medieval and early modern Science*. New York, 1959.

CUNNINGHAM, W., *Alien Immigrants to England*. London, 1897.

DAUMAS, M., *Les instruments scientifiques au XVIIe et XVIIIe siècles*. Paris, 1953.

DAVARI, S., Notizie storiche intorno al pubblico orologio di Mantova, in *Atti e Memorie della R. Accademia Virgiliana di Mantova* 1884, pp. 211-27.

DEFOSSEZ, L., *Les savants du XVIIe siècle et la mésure du temps*. Lausanne 1946.

DE GUIGNES, see GUIGNES.

DE LABORDE, see LABORDE.

DE LESPINASSE, see LESPINASSE.

D'ELIA, L., *Fonti Ricciane*. Rome, 1942-9.

DELISLE, L., *Mandements et actes divers de Charles V (1364-1380)* (Collection de Documents inédits sur l'Histoire de France). Paris, 1874.

DE PISAN, Ch., see PISAN.

DERMIGNY, L., *La Chine et l'Occident: le commerce à Canton au XVIII siècle* 1719-1833. Paris, 1964.

DERMIGNY, L., *Les Mémoires de Charles de Constant sur le commerce à la Chine*. Paris, 1964

DE SAINT EXUPÉRY, A., *Wind, Sand and Stars*. New York, 1939.

DE SOLLA PRICE, see SOLLA PRICE.

DEVELLE, E., *Les Horlogers Blésois au XVIe et au XVIIe siècle* (2nd edn.). Blois, 1917.

DIJKSTERHUIS, E. J., *The mechanisation of the World picture*. Oxford, 1961.

DOBEL, P., *Sept années en Chine*. Paris, 1842.

DONDI DALL'OROLOGIO, G., *Tractatus Astrarii* (ed. A. Barzon, E. Morpurgo, A. Petrucci, G. Francescato), Codices ex ecclesiasticis Italiae Bibliothecis selecti, vol. 9. Rome (Città del Vaticano), 1960.

DOREN A., *Deutsche Handwerker und Handwerkerbruderschaften in mittelalterlichen Italien.* Berlin, 1903.

DOUËT-D'ARCQ, L., *Comptes de l'hôtel des Rois de France au XIVe et XVe siècles.* Paris, 1865.

DU BOURG, see BOURG.

DUBY, G., *L'économie rurale et la vie des campagnes dans l'Occident médiéval.* Paris, 1962.

DUBY, G., Le problème des techniques agricoles, in *Agricoltura e mondo rurale in Occidente nell'alto medioevo.* Spoleto, 1966.

DUHALDE, J. B., *The general history of China.* London, 1741.

DUYVENDAK, J. L., The last Dutch Embassy to the Chinese Court (1794-5) in *T'oung Pao*, 34 (1939), pp. 1-137.

DUYVENDAK, J. L., Supplementary documents on the last Dutch Embassy to the Chinese Court, in *T'oung Pao*, 35 (1940), pp. 340-8.

ENSHOFF, D., Riccis Uhren, in *Die Katolischen Missionen*, 65 (1937), pp. 190-4.

L'excellence de l'horlogerie (by I.B.). Geneva, 1689.

FALCONET, Dissertation sur les anciennes horloges et sur Jacques Dondi, surnommé Horologius, in *Collection des meilleurs dissertations, notices et traités particuliers relatifs à l'histoire de France* (ed. C. Leber), vol. 16 (Paris 1838), pp. 384-409.

FALLET-SCHEURER, M., *Geschichte der Uhrmacherkunst in Basel 1370-1874.* Bern, 1917.

FANFANI, A., *Storia del lavoro in Italia dalla fine del sec. XV agli inizi del XVIII.* Milano, 1943.

FASANO-GUARINI, E., Comment naviguent les galères in *Annales E.S.C.*, 16 (1961), pp. 279-96.

FILLET, Les horloges publiques dans le Sud-Est de la France, in *Bulletin Archéologique du Comité des Travaux Historiques et Scientifiques*, 20 (1902), pp. 101-19.

FINLEY, M. I., Technical Innovation and Economic Progress in the Ancient World, in *The Economic History Review*, ser. 2, vol. 18 (1965), pp. 29-45.

FLEMING, J. A., *Flemish influence in Britain.* Glasgow, 1930.

FRANKLIN, A., *La vie privée d'autrefois*, vol. 4: *La mésure du temps.* Paris, 1888.

FRANKLIN, A., *Dictionnaire historique des arts, métiers et professions exercés dans Paris depuis le treizième siècle.* Paris-Leipzig, 1906.

FRIESE, H., Zum Aufstieg von Handwerken ins Beamtentum während der Ming-Zeit, in *Oriens Extremus*, 6 (1959), pp. 161-72.

FRISCHHOLZ, G., Nürnberg in der Geschichte der Uhren, in *Deutsche Uhrmacher-Zeitung*, 21, pp. 252-60.

FROISSART, J., *Li Orloge Amoureuses*, in *Oeuvres de Froissart, Poésies*, ed. A. Scheler, Bruxelles 1870-2, vol. 1, pp. 53-86.

FRYKE, Chr., A relation of a voyage made to the East Indies (1680-86) in *Voyages to the East Indies* (ed. C. E. Fayle). London, 1929.

GALLIOT, H., *Le métier d'horloger en Franche-Comté des origines à 1900* (Thése 1954, dactyl.—copy at the Université de Paris— Faculté de Droit).

GARZONI, T., *La Piazza Universale di tutte le professioni del mondo.* Venice, 1595.

GATTY, A., *The Book of Sun-dials* (eds. H. K. F. Gatty and E. Lloyd). London, 1889.

GEANAKOPLOS, D. J., A Byzantine look at the Renaissance: the attitude of Michael Apostolis toward the rise of Italy to cultural eminence, in *Greek and Byzantine Studies*, 1 (1958), pp. 157-62.

GEISENDORF, P. F., Métiers et conditions sociales du premier Refuge à Geneve (1549-1587) in *Mélanges d'histoire économique et sociale en hommage au professeur Antony Babel*, Geneva 1963, vol. 1, pp. 239-49.

GÉLIS, E., *L'Horlogerie ancienne.* Paris 1949.

GÉNICOT, L., On the evidence of Growth of Population in the West from the Eleventh to the Thirteenth Century, in *Change in Medieval Society* (ed. S. L. Thrupp), New York, 1964, pp. 14-29.

GEORGE, D., *London Life in the Eighteenth Century.* London, 1925.

GIERSBERG, J., Kölner Uhrmacher im 15 bis 19 Jahrhundert in *Beitrage zur Kölnischen Geschichte*—Sprache, vol. 1, no. 4 (Mai 1915), pp. 274-91.

BIBLIOGRAPHY

GLORIA, A., L'orologio di Jacopo Dondi nella Piazza dei Signori in Padova, in *Atti e Memorie della R. Accademia di Scienze, Lettere ed Arti in Padova*, 286 (1885), pp. 233-93.

GRÉSY, E., Inventaire des objets d'art composant la succession de Florimond Robertet, ministre de François Ier, in *Mémoires de la Société Impériale des Antiquaires de France*, vol. 30 (1868), pp. 1-66.

GRISELINI, F., *Dizionario delle arti e de' mestieri*, ed. M. Fossadoni. Venice, 1771.

GUICCIARDINI, F., Relazione di Spagna (1512-13), in *Opere* (R. Palmarocchi ed.), Bari 1936.

DE GUIGNES, J. C. L., *Voyages à Peking, Manille et l'Ile de France*. Paris, 1808.

GÜMBEL, A., *Peter Henlein, der Erfinder der Taschenuhren*, Halle, 1924.

HALL, A. R., The Scholar and the Craftsman in the Scientific Revolution, in *Critical Problems in the History of Science* (ed. M. Clagett), Madison, Wisc., 1959.

HAMILTON, H., *The English Brass and Copper Industries to 1800*. London, 1926.

HARCOURT-SMITH, S., *A Catalogue of Various clocks, watches, automata and other Miscellaneous objects of European workmanship dating from the XVIIIth and the early XIXth centuries in the Palace Museum and the Wu Ying Tien, Peiping*. Peiping, 1933.

HAUSER, F., and E. WIEDEMANN, see WIEDEMANN.

HENRARD, P., Documents pour servir à l'histoire de l'artillerie en Belgique. Les fondeurs d'artillerie, in *Annales de l'Académie d'Archéologie de Belgique*, 45 (1889), pp. 237-81.

HENSLOW, T. G. W., *Ye Sundial Booke*. London 1914.

Histoire de l'Academie Royale des Inscriptions et belles-lettres. Paris, 1736.

HO, Ping-Ti, *The Ladder of Success in Imperial China. Aspects of Social Mobility 1368-1911*. New York, 1964.

HO, Ping-Ti, *Studies on the Population of China 1368-1953*. Cambridge (Mass.), 1959.

HOGG, W., *The Book of old sundials and their mottoes*. London, Edinburgh, Boston, 1917.

HOOGEWERFF, G. J., *De geschiedenis van de St. Lucasgilden in Nederland*. Amsterdam, 1947.

HORSKÝ, Z. and E. PROCHÁZKA, Pražský Orloj. in *Acta Historiae Rerum Naturalium nec non Technicarum* 9 (Prague, 1964), pp. 83-146.

Instructions sublimes et familaires de Cheng-Tzu-Quogen-Hoang-Ti, in *Mémoires concernant l'histoire, les sciences, les arts, les moeurs, les usages etc. des Chinois par les missionaires de Pekin*, vol. 9. Paris, 1783.

JAQUET and CHAPUIS, A., *Histoire et technique de la Montre Suisse de ses origines à nos jours*. Basel, 1945.

JONES, R. F., *Ancients and Moderns* (Washington University Studies. N.S. Language and Literature, no. 6). St. Louis, 1936.

KAEMPFER, E., *The history of Japan together with a description of the kingdom of Siam 1690-2* (ed. J. G. Scheuchzer). Glasgow, 1906.

KELLER, A. G., A Byzantine admirer of 'Western' progress: Cardinal Bessarion, in *Cambridge Historical Journal*, 11 (1955), pp. 343-8.

KISTNER, A., *Die Schwarzwälder Uhr*. Karlsruhe, 1927.

KURZ, O., *European Clocks and Watches in the Near East*. Warburg, 1976.

LABARTE, J. (ed.), Inventaire du mobilier de Charles V, rois de France, in *Collection de Documents inédits sur l'histoire de France*, Ser. III. Paris, 1879.

de LABORDE, *Notice des émaux, bijoux et objets divers exposés dans les Galéries du Musée du Louvre*. Paris, 1853.

LAMALLE, E., La propagande du P. Nicolas Trigault en faveur des missions de Chine (1616), in *Archivum Historicum Societatis Jesu* 9 (1940), pp. 49-120.

LAMBROS, S. P., Ipomnima tou Kardinaliou Vissarionos, in *Neos Hellenomnemon*, 3 (1906), pp. 15-27.

LECOCQ, A., Notice historique et archeologique sur les horloges de Chartres, in *Mémoires de la Société Archéologique d'Eure et Loire*, 4 (1867), pp. 284-340.

LE COMTE, L., *Empire of China*. London, 1737.

LE GOFF, J., Au Moyen Age: temps de l'Église et temps du marchand, in *Annales, E.S.C.*, 15 (1960), pp. 417-33.

LE GOFF, J., Le Temps du Travail dans la crise du XIVe siècle:

du temps médiéval au temps moderne, in *Le Moyen Age*, 69 (1963), pp. 597-613.

DE LESPINASSE, R., *Les métiers et corporations de la Ville de Paris* (Coll. Histoire Générale de Paris). Paris, 1886-97.

LEWIS, A., The Closing of the Medieval Frontier, in *Speculum*, 33 (1958).

LIISBERG, B., *Urmagare og Ure i Danmark*. Copenhagen, 1908.

van LINSCHOTEN, J. H., *The Voyage to the East Indies*, ed. by A. C. Burnell and P. A. Tiele. London, 1885.

LLOYD, H. A., *Giovanni de Dondi's Horological Masterpiece of A.D. 1364*. London (priv. pr.), 1954.

LLOYD, H. A., *Some outstanding clocks over seven hundred years 1250-1950*. London, 1958.

LOPEZ, R. S., Venezia e le grandi linee dell'espansione commerciale nel sec. XIII, in *La Civiltà Veneziana del secolo di Marco Polo*, Venice, 1955, pp. 37-82.

LOPEZ, R. S., L'extrème frontière du commerce de l'Europe médiévale, in *Le Moyen Age*, 69 (1963), pp. 479-90.

LUNDWALL, S., *Stjärnsundsuren Väggurtillverkningen vid ett 1700-tals bruk*. Stockholm 1949.

LUZZATTO, G., Cenni intorno alla vita e alle opere storiche di Girolamo Brusoni, in *Ateneo Veneto*, 21 (1898), pp. 273-305 and 22 (1899), pp. 6-26 and 226-44.

MANETTI, A., *Vita di Filippo di ser Brunellesco* (ed. E. Toesca). Florence, 1927.

MARIANI, M., *Vita Universitaria Pavese nel secolo XV*. Pavia 1899.

MICHEL, H., L'Horloge de Sapience et l'histoire de l'horlogerie, in *Physis*, 2 (1960), pp. 291-8.

MICHEL, R., Les prémières horloges du Palais Pontifical d'Avignon, in *Mélanges d'Archéologie et d'Histoire de l'École Française de Rome*, 29 (1909), pp. 213-24.

MICLET, P., L'horloge de la Cathédrale de Beauvais; son auteur, le chanoine Étienne Musique, in *Mémoires de la Société académique de l'Oise*, 22 (1913), pp. 237-56.

MONREAL Y TEYADA, L., *Relojes antiguos (1500-1850): colecion F. Perez de Olaguer-Felieu*. Barcelona, 1955.

MORPURGO, E., *L'origine dell'orologio tascabile*. Rome, 1954.

MORPURGO, E., *L'orologio e il pendolo*. Rome, 1957

MORPURGO, E. *Dizionario degli orologiai italiani*. Rome, 1950.

MORPURGO, E., Una bottega di orologiai del Quattrocento, in *La Clessidra*, 15 (January 1959).

MORPURGO, E., Alcuni appunti sugli orologiai della Volpaia, in *La Clessidra*, 15 (September 1959), pp. 23-6.

MORPURGO, E., Sul contributo dei meccanici italiani nel campo della piccola orologeria, in *Physis*, 3 (1961), p. 166.

MORPURGO, E., Raffronto tra l'Astrario e il Planetario del Dondi, in *La Clessidra*, 19 (September 1962), pp. 37-46.

MORPURGO, E., Ruote o molle? in *La Clessidra*, 21 (September 1965), pp. 31-2.

MORSE, H. B., *The Chronicles of the East India Company Trading to China 1635-1834*. Cambridge, Mass., 1926.

MORYSON, F., *Itinerary* (ed. C. Hughes). London, 1903.

MOTTA, E., Musici alla Corte degli Sforza, in *Archivio Storico Lombardo*, 14 (1887), pp. 29-64; 278-340; 514-61.

MURATORI, L. A., *Dissertazioni sopra le Antichità Italiane*. Milan, 1751.

MURATORI, L. A., *Rerum Italicarum Scriptores*. Milan, 1723-1770.

N.N., Tedeschi in Milano nel Quattrocento, in *Archivio Storico Lombardo*, 19 (1892), pp. 996-9.

N.N., Das Augsburger Uhrmachergewerbe in *Augsburger Rundschau*, 4 (January, 14, 1922), pp. 205ff.

N.N., *Relojes del Patrimonio Nacional*. Barcelona, 1965.

N.N., Un eccezionale orologio del 1585 appartenuto al Re di Svezia, in *La Clessidra*, 21 (November 1965), p. 43.

NEEDHAM, J., *Science and Civilization in China*. Cambridge, 1954ff.

NEEDHAM, J., WANG LING, and D. J. DE SOLLA PRICE, *Heavenly Clockwork*. Cambridge, 1960.

NEEDHAM, J., Poverties and Triumphs of the Chinese Scientific Tradition, in *Scientific Change*, ed. A. C. Crombie, London, 1963, pp. 117-53.

NIEUHOFF, J., *An Embassy to China* (1655). London, 1669.

OLDEWELT, W. F. H., De beroepsstructuur van de bevolking der Hollandse stemhebbende steden volgens de Kohieren van de familiegelden van 1674, 1715 en 1742, in *Economisch Historisch Jaarboek* 24 (1950), pp. 80-161.

OLSCHKI, L., *Guillaume Boucher, a French artist at the court of the Khans*. Baltimore, 1946.

ORNSTEIN, M., *The rôle of the scientific societies in the seventeenth century*. New York, 1913.

OSBECK, P., *A Voyage to China and the East Indies*. London, 1771.

OTTEMA, N., *Geschiedenis van de uurwerkmakerskunst in Friesland*, Assen, 1948.

P.P., L'orologio dell'Ospedale Maggiore di Milano nel sec. XV, in *Archivio Storico Lombardo*, 44 (1917), pp. 687-8.

PAGE, W. (ed.), *The Victoria History of the County of Middlesex*. London, 1911.

PANIKKAR, K. M., *Asia and Western Dominance*. London, 1961.

PEATE, I. C., *Clock and watch makers in Wales*. Cardiff, 1945.

PELLIOTT, P., Bulletin Critique (review of A. Chapuis, *La Montre Chinoise*), in *T'oung Pao*, ser. 2, vol. 20 (1920-21), pp. 61-8.

PFISTER, L., *Notices biographiques et bibliographiques sur les Jésuites de l'ancienne mission de Chine*. Shanghai, 1932

PHOLIEN, F., *L'Horlogerie et ses Artistes au Pays de Liége*. Liége, 1933.

PIERIS, P.E., and M. A. H. FITZLER, *Ceylon and Portugal* Leipzig, 1927.

PIRENNE, H., *Historie de la Belgique*. Bruxelles, 1911.

DE PISAN, CH., Le livre des fais et bonnes meurs du sage Roy Charles V, in *Nouvelle Collection des Mémoires pour servir à l'histoire de France*, vols. 1 and 2, Paris, 1836.

PLANCHON, M., *L'Horloge, son histoire retrospective*. Paris, 1925.

POHL, H., *L'Homme à la poursuite du temps* Paris, 1957.

PRODAN, M., *Chinese Art*. New York, 1958.

RACHEL, H., *Das Berliner Wirtschaftsleben im Zeitalter des Frühkapitalismus*. Berlin, 1931.

RAYNAUD, G., Paris en 1596 vu par un Italien, in *Bulletin de la Société de l'Histoire de Paris et de l'Ile-de-France*, 12 (1885), pp. 164-70.

RENIER, R., Gaspare Visconti, in *Archivio Storico Lombardo*, 13 (1886), pp. 509-62 and 777-824.

RETI, L., Francesco di Giorgio Martini's Treatise on Engineering and its Plagiarists, in *Technology and Culture*, 4 (1963), pp. 287-98.

REVERCHON, L., *Petite histoire de l'Horlogerie*. Besançon, s.d.

ROBERTSON, J. D., *The Evolution of Clockwork with a special section on the Clocks of Japan*. London, 1931.

ROSSI, P., *I filosofi e le macchine* Milan, 1962.

RUBBIANI, A., L'orologio del comune di Bologna e la sfera del 1451, in *Atti e Memorie della R. Deputazione di Storia Patria per le Provincie di Romagna*, ser. 3, vol. 26 (1908), pp. 349-66.

SANDOZ, CH., *Les Horloges et les maîtres horlogeurs à Besançon du XVe siècle à la Révolution Française*. Besançon 1905.

SARREIRA, R., Horas boas e horas más para a civilização chinesa, in *Broteria*, 36 (1943), pp. 518-28.

SAVARY, J., *Dictionnaire universel du Commerce*. Copenhagen, 1761.

SAY, J. B., *Cours complet d'économie politique*. Bruxelles, 1840.

SCITOVSKY, T., *Papers on Welfare and Growth*. London, 1964.

SCHADE, F., *Uhrmacher Lexicon*. Weimar, 1855.

SCHENK, A., *Die Uhrmacher von Winterthur und ihre Werke*. Winterthur, 1958.

SCHULTHEIS, W., Peter Henlein. *Nürnberger Gestalten aus neun Jahrhunderten* (Nürnberg 1950), pp. 91-4.

SCHURZ, W. L., *The Manila Galleon*. New York, 1959.

SCOVILLE, W. C., *The Persecution of Huguenots and French economic development, 1680-1720*. Berkeley-Los Angeles 1960.

SELLERGREN, G., Polhem's Contributions to Applied Mechanics, in *Christopher Polhem the father of Swedish Technology*. Hartford, Conn., 1963.

SEVCENKO, I., The Decline of Byzantium seen through the eyes of its Intellectuals, in *Dumbarton Oaks Papers*, 15 (1961), pp. 167-86.

SHELDON, C. D., *The rise of the Merchant Class in Tokugawa Japan 1600-1868*. Ann Arbor, 1958.

SIDENBLADH, E., *Urmakare i Sverige under äldre tider*, Nordiska Museets Handlingar, 28. Stockholm, 1947.

SIMONI, A., Un orologio a cembalo in una miniatura quattrocentesca, in *La Clessidra*, 21 (November 1965), pp. 40-2.

SLICHER VAN BATH, B. H., *The Agrarian History of Western Europe, A.D. 500-1850*. London, 1963.

SMITH, A., *The Wealth of Nations*. New York, 1937.

SMITH, J., *Old Scottish Clockmakers*. Edinburgh, 1921.

DE SOLLA PRICE, D. J., On the origin of clockwork, perpetual motion and the compass, in *U.S. National Museum Bulletin* 218 (Washington, 1959), pp. 82-112.

DE SOLLA PRICE, D. J., Mechanical water clocks of the fourteenth century in Fez, Morocco, in *Actes du I Congrès International d'Histoire des Sciences*, Paris, 1964, vol. 1, pp. 599-601.

DE SOLLA PRICE, D. J., Automata and the origins of mechanism and mechanistic Philosophy, in *Technology and Culture*, 5 (1964), pp. 9-23.

DE SOLLA PRICE, D. J., *Science since Babylon*. New Haven and London, 1961.

STONE, L., State control in sixteenth-century England in *Economic History Review*, vol. 17 (1947), pp. 103-20.

SYMONDS, R. W., *A History of English Clocks*. London-New York, 1947.

TAEUBER, I. B., *The Population of Japan*. Princeton, 1958.

TAKABASHI, H., *Tokei Hattatzu shi*. Tokyo, 1924.

THOMAS, P. J., *Mercantilism and the East India Trade*. London, 1963.

THORNDIKE, L., *A History of Magic and Experimental Science*. New York, 1934.

THORNDIKE, L., Milan manuscripts of Giovanni de Dondi's astronomical clock and of Jacopo de Dondi's discussion of tides, in *Archeion*, 18 (1936), pp. 308-17.

THORNDIKE, L., Invention of the mechanical clock about A.D. 1271, in *Speculum*, 16 (1941), pp. 242-3.

TSUKADA, T., *Wadokei*. Tokyo, 1960.

ULLYETT, K., *British Clocks and Clockmakers*. London, 1947.

UNGERER, A. and TH., *L'Horloge astronomique de la Cathédrale de Strasbourg*. Strasbourg, 1922.

UNGERER, A., *Les horloges astronomiques et monumentales les plus remarquables de l'Antiquité jusqu' à nos jours*. Strasbourg 1931.

UNGERER, T., Les Habrechts: une dynastie d'horlogers strasbourgeois aux XVIe et XVIIe siècles in *Archives alsaciennes d'histoire de l'art*. Strasbourg, 1925.

Urkundenbuch der Stadt Strassburg (ed. H. Witte), vol. 7 of the Urkunden und Akten der Stadt Strassburg. Strasbourg, 1900.

USHER, A. P., *A History of Mechanical Inventions*. Boston, 1959.

van Braam, see BRAAM.

van Linschoten, see LINSCHOTEN.

van Werveke, see WERVEKE.

VASARI, *Le vite dei più eccellenti pittori, scultori, e architetti*, (ed. C. L. Ragghianti), Milan-Rome, 1942-9.

VENTURI, F., *Le origini dell'Enciclopedia*. Torino, 1963.

VERBIEST, F., *Astronomia Europea sub Imperatore Tartaro—Sinico Cam-Hy*. Dillingen, 1687.

VIAL, E., and C. CÔTE, *Les Horlogers Lyonnais de 1550 à 1650* Lyon, 1927.

VIDIER, A., Les gouverneurs de l'horloge du Palais, in *Bulletin de la Société de l'histoire de Paris et de l'Ile-de-France*, 38 (1911), pp. 95-103.

Vie de Saint Louis par le Confesseur de la Reine Marguerite, in *Recueil des Historiens des Gaules et de la France*, vol. 20 (Paris, 1840), pp. 58-121.

VIELLIARD, J., Horloges et Horlogers catalans á la fin du Moyen Age, in *Bulletin Hispanique*, 63 (1961), pp. 161-8.

Von Bassermann-Jordan E., see BASSERMANN.

Von Bertele, see BERTELE.

WÄHLIN, TH., *Horologium mirabile Lundense*. Lund, 1923.

WARD, F. A. B., *Time Measurement*. London, 1958.

WEBER, H., *La Compagnie Française des Indes (1604-1875)*. Paris 1904.

Van WERVEKE, A., L'Horloge in *La Flandre Libérale*, 25 March 1932, reprinted in *Gedenkbladen uit het leven onzer voorouders*. Ghent, 1936, pp. 209-13.

WHITE, L., *Medieval Technology and Social Change*. Oxford, 1963.

WIEDEMANN, E., and F. HAUSER, *Ueber die Uhren im Bereich der Islamischen Kultur*. Halle, 1915.

WIENER, P. P., and A. NOLAND (eds.), *Roots of Scientific Thought.* New York, 1960.

WRIGHT, F. A. (ed. and transla.), *The Works of Liudprand of Cremona.* London, 1930.

ZINNER, E., *Die Ältesten Räderuhren und Modernen Sonnenuhren,* Bericht der Naturforschenden Geselleschaft 28. Bamberg, 1939.

ZINNER, E., *Aus der Frühzeit der Räderuhr von der Gewichtsuhr zur Federzugsuhr,* Deutsches Museum—Abhandlungen und Berichte 22. München, 1954.

ZINNER, E., *Deutsche und Niederländische Astronomische Instrumente, des 11-18 Jahrhunderts.* München, 1956.

ZINNER, E., Die Augsburger Uhrmacherei von 1550 bis 1650, in *Neue Uhrmacher-Zeitung,* 12 (1958), *n.* 16, pp. 27-34.

ZINNER, E., Wurde die Räderuhr in Deutschland oder in Italien erfunden, in *Die Himmelswelt,* 53 (1943), pp. 17-22.

INDEX

Abel, Clarke, English traveller and naturalist, *quoted*, 90

Abu'l-Ala al Ma'arri, Arab writer, 40

Acapulco, 150

Agricola, Georg, German metallurgist, 25

Al-Jazari, Moslem encyclopaedist, 26, 117

Alberti, Leone Battista, Italian architect, 24

Alemaigne, Jehan d', German clockmaker in France, 52, 129

Alfonso I, Duke of Ferrara, 135

Alfred, King of Wessex, 119

Antwerp, decline of, 62

Arai Hakuseki, Japanese official, 160

Archimedes, Greek mathematician, 20, 87

Arnold, John, English clockmaker, 56, 137, 157

Asser, English bishop and biographer, 119

Astronomus, Petrus, German clockmaker in Sweden, 128

Augsburg, clock industry in, 53, 61, 62, 64, 132, 139, 140

Bach, Johann Sebastian, German musician and composer, 101

Baden, clock industry in, 72

Barlow, Edward, English clockmaker, 69

Baroccio ——, Italian clockmaker, 140

Barrow, John, *quoted*, 91, 93-4, 160, 161-2, 164

Bartolomeo di Gnudolo, Italian clockmaker, 44

Bayard, Master, French clockmaker in Geneva, 64

Beethoven, Ludwig van, German musical composer, 101

Beliard, ——, *quoted*, 74

bells, rôle in medieval society, 38

Berlin, clock industry in, 51, 72

Besançon, clock industry in, 122, 129, 135, 148

Bessarion, Joanes, Cardinal (Patriarch of Constantinople), 26, *quoted*, 27-8, 32, 44

Besson, Jacques, French mathematician, 25

Biringuccio, Vanuccio, Italian mathematician and metallurgist, 24

19TH AND 20TH CENTURY EUROPEAN HISTORY IN
NORTON PAPERBACK

Schoenbaum, David. *Hitler's Social Revolution: Class and Status in Nazi Germany, 1933–1939.* N993

Sontag, Raymond James. *Germany and England: Background of Conflict, 1848–1894.* N180

Stearns, Peter N. *1848: The Revolutionary Tide in Europe.* 9311

Talmon, J. L. *The Origins of Totalitarian Democracy.* N510

Talmon, R. R. *Romanticism and Revolt, 1815–1848.* 95081

Taylor, A. J. P. *Germany's First Bid for Colonies, 1884–1885.* N530

Turner, L. C. F. *Origins of the First World War.* 9947

von der Mehden, Fred R. *South-East Asia 1930–1970: The Legacy of Colonialism and Nationalism.* 9320

Waite, Robert G. L. *Vanguard of Nazism: The Free Corps Movement in Postwar Germany, 1918–1923.* N181

Weber, Eugen. *Europe Since 1715: A Modern History.* 9404

Wheeler-Bennett, John W. *Brest-Litovsk: The Forgotten Peace, March 1918.* N576

Wheeler-Bennett, John W. and Anthony Nicholls. *The Semblance of Peace: The Political Settlement After the Second World War.* N709

Whyte, A. J. *The Evolution of Modern Italy.* N298

Williams, Roger L. *The French Revolution of 1870–1871.* 9837

Wolfers, Arnold. *Britain and France between Two Wars.* N343

Wolff, Robert Lee. *The Balkans in Our Time.* (New Ed.) 9010

Wright, Gordon. *France in Modern Times.* (3d Ed.) 95153

THE NORTON HISTORY OF
MODERN EUROPE

Rice, Eugene F., Jr. *The Foundations of Early Modern Europe, 1460–1559.*

Dunn, Richard S. *The Age of Religious Wars, 1559–1689.* (2d Ed.)

Krieger, Leonard. *Kings and Philosophers, 1689–1789.*

Breunig, Charles. *The Age of Revolution and Reaction, 1789–1850.* (2d Ed.)

Rich, Norman. *The Age of Nationalism and Reform, 1850–1890.* (2d Ed.)

Gilbert, Felix. *The End of the European Era, 1890 to the Present.* (2d Ed.)